CHARLIE BURK

JOURNEY IN ABSTRACTION

FRESCO BOOKS

Publisher
SF Design, llc / Fresco Books
Albuquerque, NM
www.frescobooks.com

Foreword by Nick Abdalla
Introduction by Karla Winterowd
Essays by Claudia Joseph and Iris McLister

Design by Nancy Stem, Fresco Books
Photographs by Pat Berrett
Portrait photographs by James Holbrook
Cover photograph by Gary Mankus Studios

Cover image: *Into the Wonder* (detail)

Composed in Avenir LT Std.
Measurements are provided in inches unless otherwise noted.

Library of Congress Control Number: 2018947205
ISBN: 978-1-934491-64-5

Paintings available: Winterowd Fine Art, Santa Fe, NM
Book distribution: University of New Mexico Press, unmpress.org
and Winterowd Fine Art

CHARLIE BURK

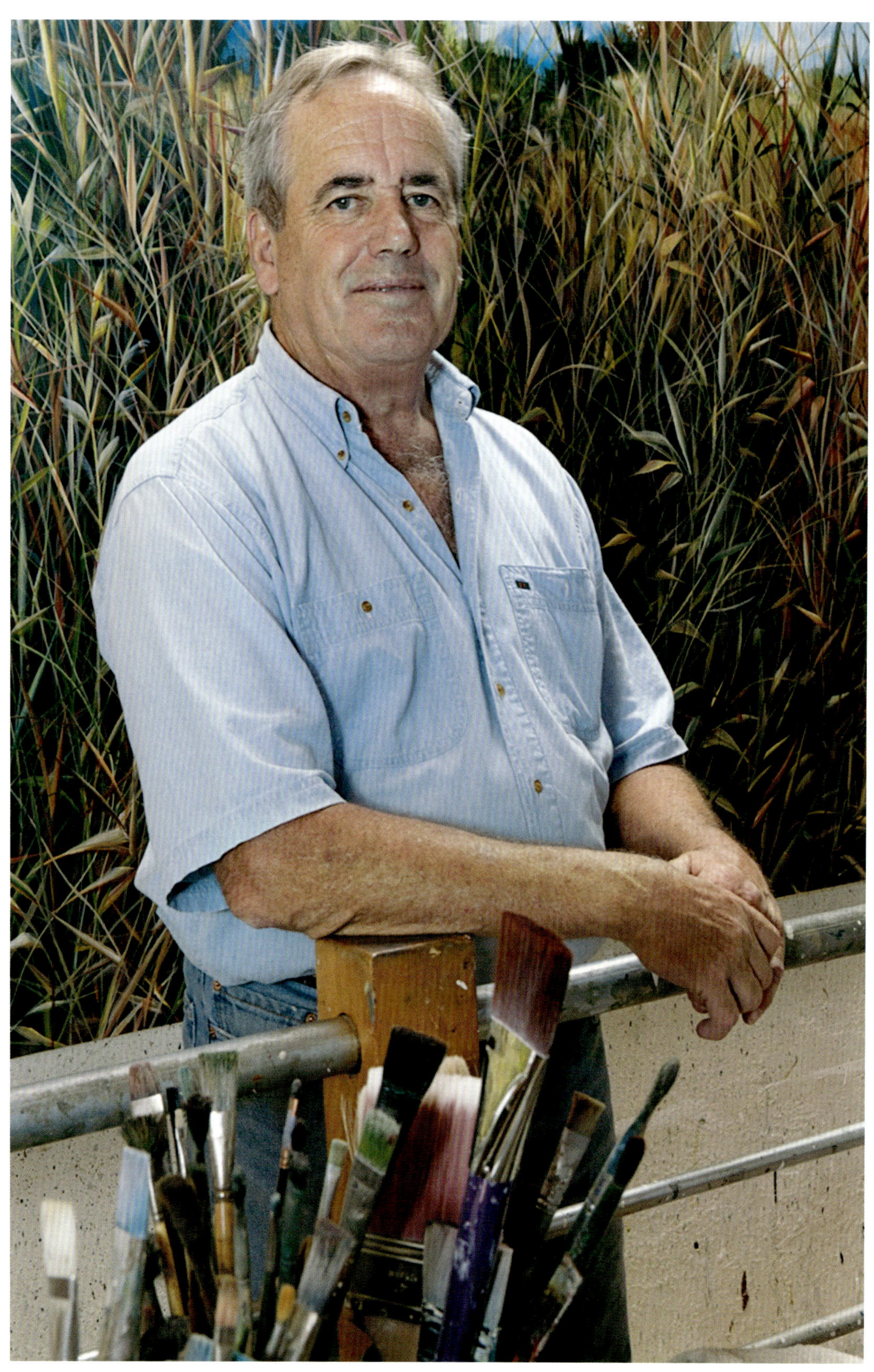

    Charlie Burk

NICK ABDALLA

The paintings Charlie Burk creates are beautiful, unique, and magical. At first glance, they seem to be totally abstract, but become amazingly super realistic the longer one views them. He paints a mundane subject matter, grass, which is ubiquitous in our environment, but seldom, if ever, the subject of artistic investigation. The works are landscapes, not in the stereotypical sense of distant vistas and romantic or dramatic lighting, but they are landscapes nonetheless. Instead of looking up and out, Burk chooses to look down—where our feet are. He asks, "What do you see?" He answers, "You see where you are. You see what is there!"

Upon closer inspection, the paintings expose a world that is microcosmic, revealing details often seen only by children crawling on the ground or by small animals and insects making their way in their world. He explores an overlooked world that transforms our view of the world around us. It is a view of a world within a world.

In examining what is there, Burk paints grass as if it were a forest, each stalk different in size, character, color, and personality. There are rhythms and paths; there is quiet and intrigue. At the top edge of a painting, a sliver of blue grounds us in the landscape, and reminds us where we are and what we have missed in our experience of the everyday world. Charlie Burk's unique vision reveals to us a quiet place in the world that goes unnoticed. His paintings embody the magic of the overlooked.

Nick Abdalla
Professor Emeritus
University of New Mexico
Department of Art and Art History

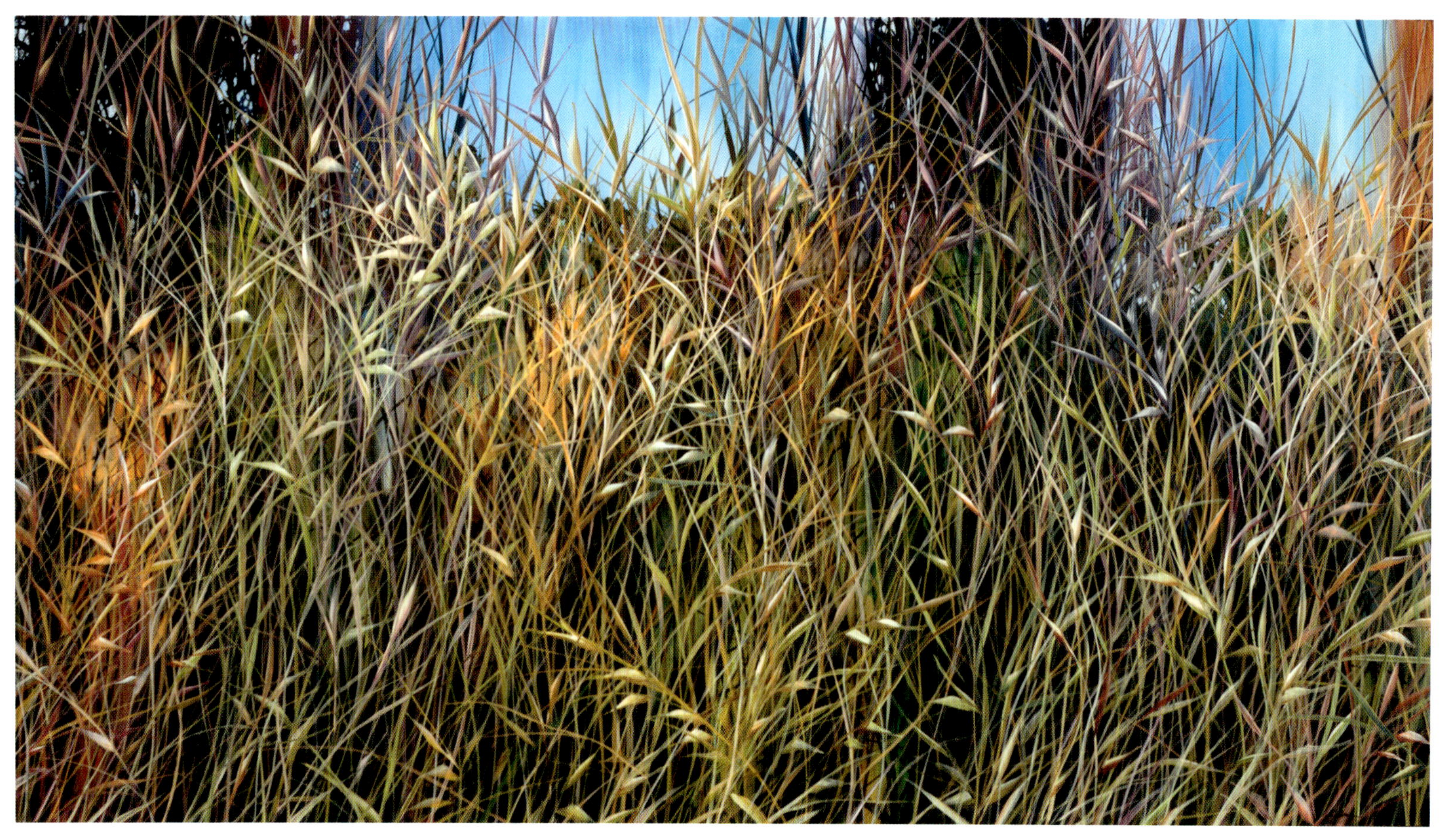

Dancing Light, 2017   40 x 72   Oil on panel
Collection of Jennifer Webb and Dean Williams

INTRODUCTION

KARLA WINTEROWD

Those of us who seek the relief and the comfort of beauty in Nature are easily drawn into the art of Charlie Burk. The artist explores an inner sanctum of an untouched world rarely explored; a private, close-up view near to the earth's surface. The paintings conjure up sounds of soft, rustling grass shifting with the wind. The upward movement of the artist's stroke evokes childhood memories of stands of grass—hiding in the reeds, rolling across grassy lawns, and delighting in the cool blades against the skin. Charlie Burk is unquestionably in touch with the pulse of the earth when he paints these masterful works of art.

Charlie has created his own rhythm in the studio by painting daily for the last forty years. His early work explored realism within the confines of the watercolor medium. He invested long periods of time with each painting, often choosing subjects unnoticed by casual observers. Ultimately Charlie Burk abandoned the watercolor medium for oil painting, taking with him skills he developed over the course of decades.

The freedom of this lush, newly chosen oil medium allowed him to explore mark-making in a new way, getting even closer to his subject. For Charlie the world of painting opened wider with the use of oil paint and he stepped out into a more exuberant practice of color, shape, texture, and movement. The closer he moved into examination of Nature the more liberated his brush became until abstraction prevailed.

For the last fifteen years, Charlie Burk has been painting with renewed joy, clarity, and vitality. Within his work there is much room to interpret and explore. His patience and skill with the materials are extraordinary. Approaching each painting as a unique expression, he lays layer upon layer of pigment, taking all the time he needs to create a *tour de force*.

Karla Winterowd
Winterowd Fine Art
Santa Fe, New Mexico

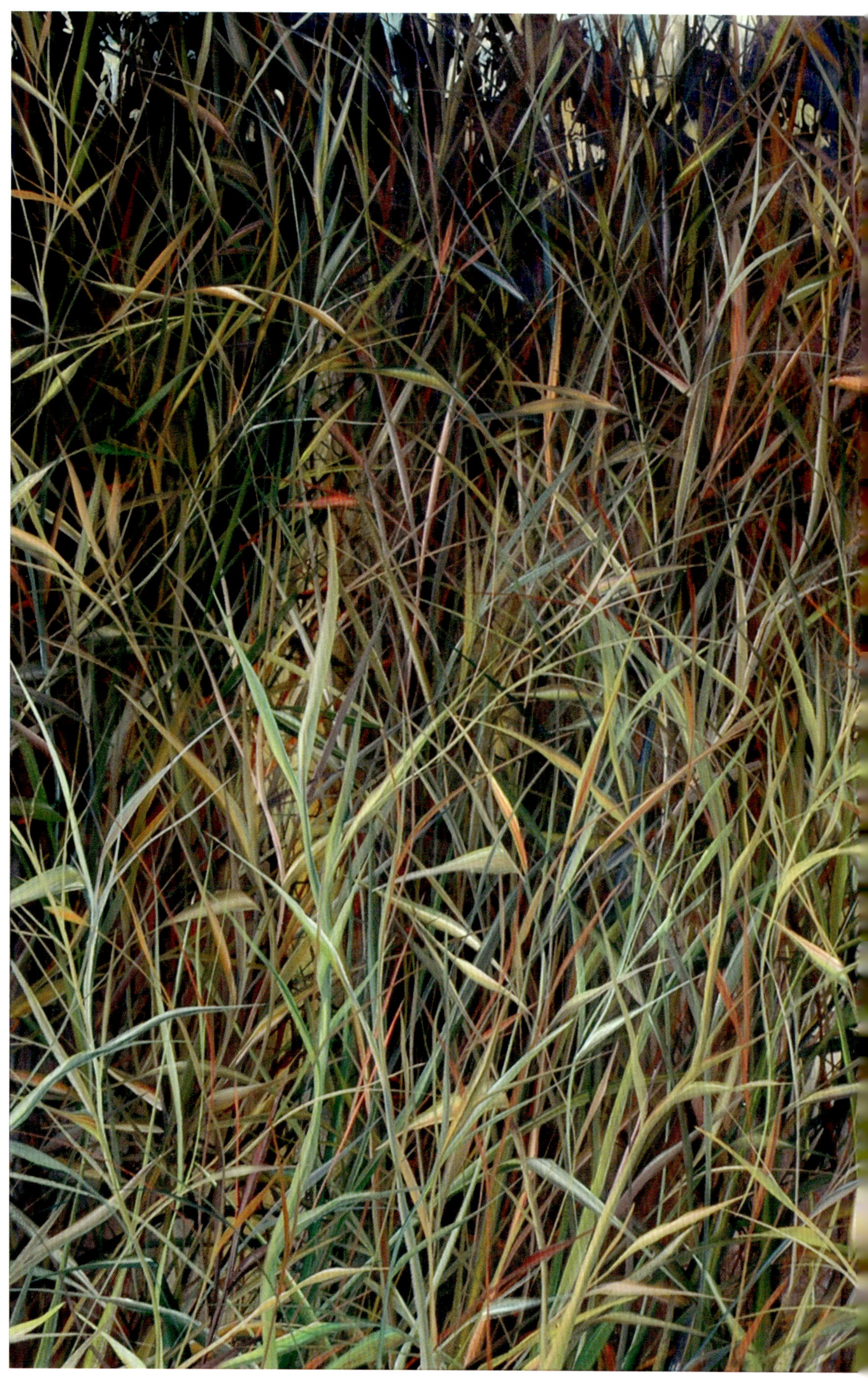

Sundance, 2012   72 x 96   Oil on canvas
Private Collection

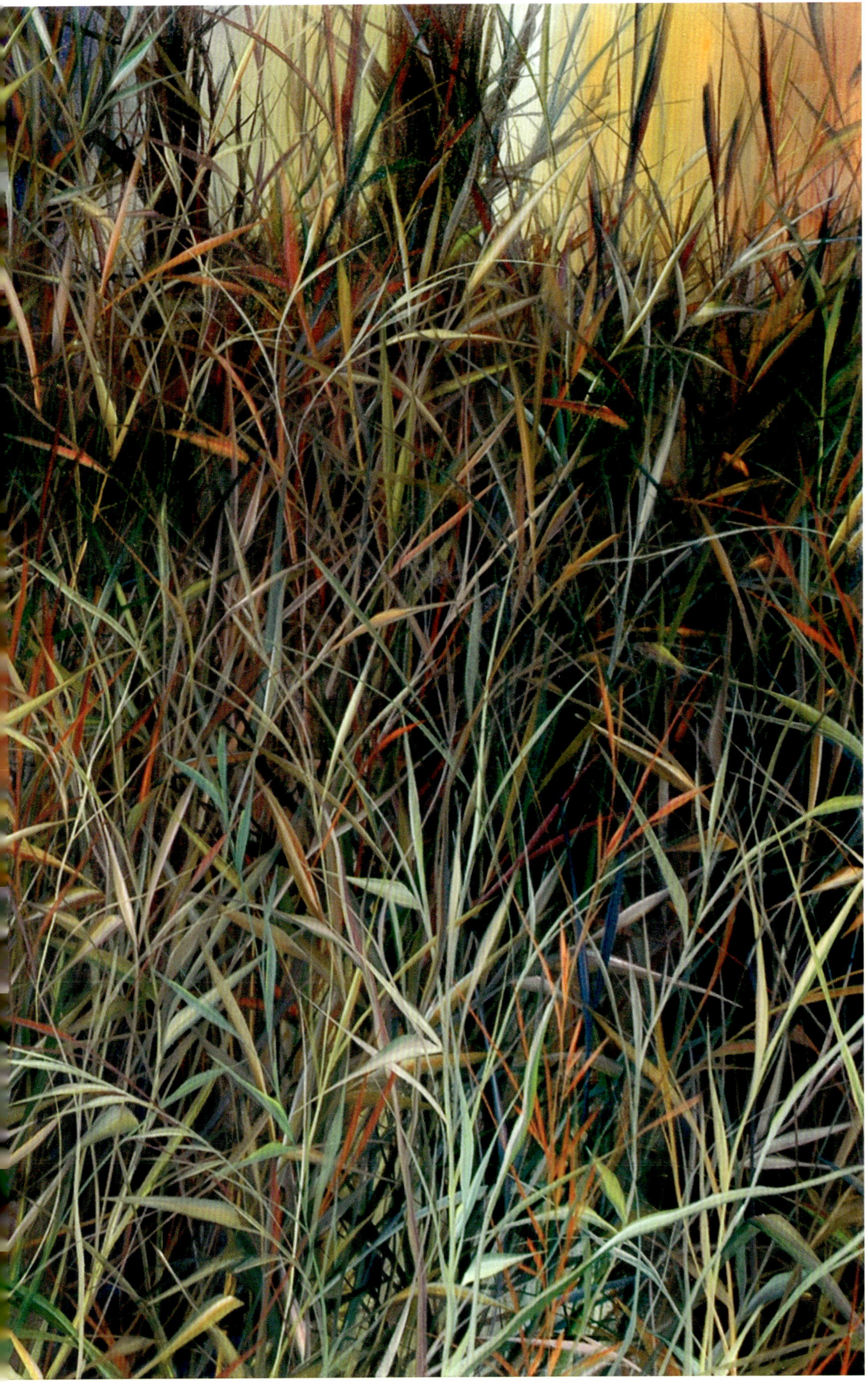

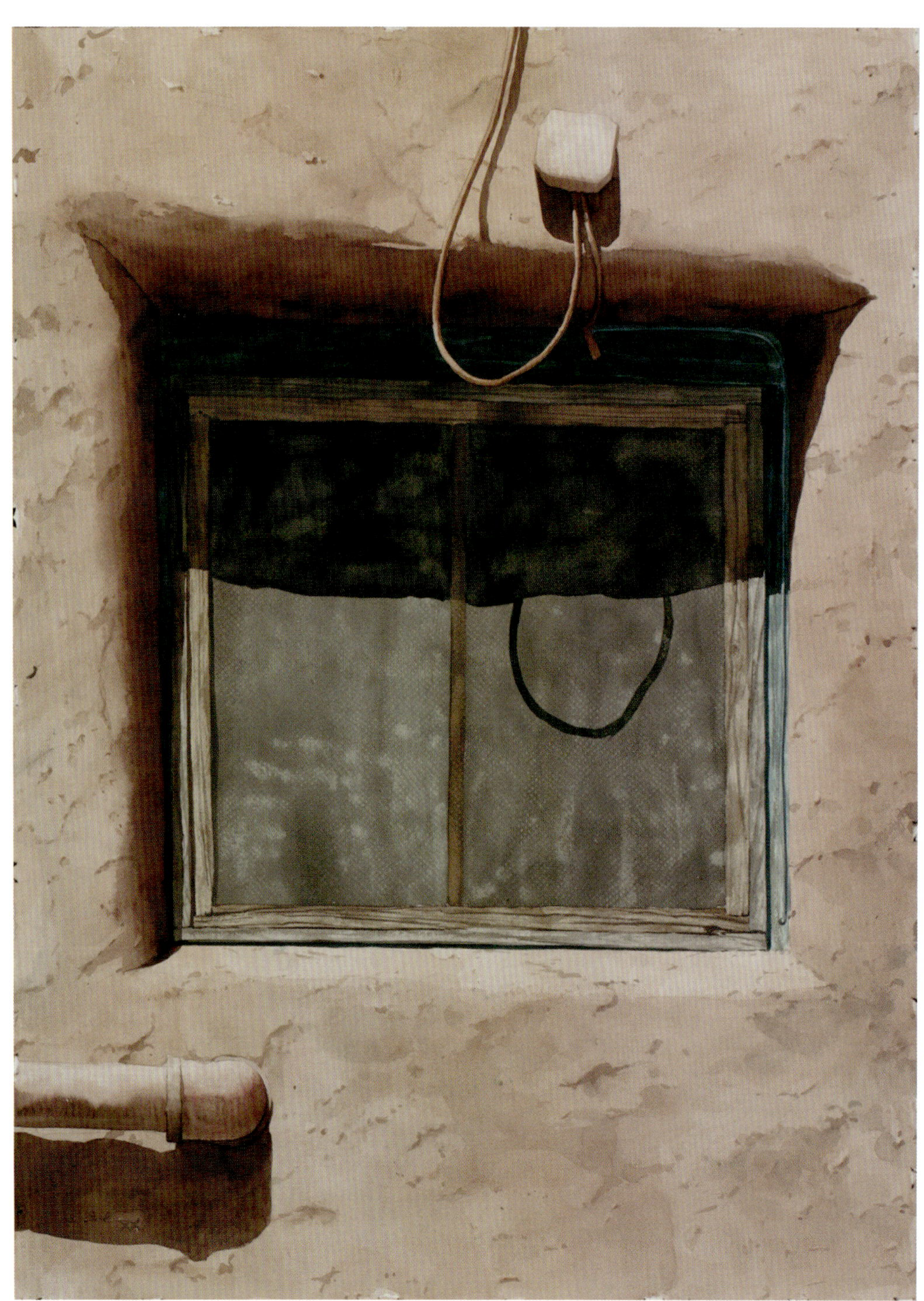

Confessional, 1992   30 x 22   Watercolor
Collection of Frances Salman Koenig

CHARLIE BURK

Most beginnings start with outside influences, those people who surround us as we grow.

My father, William E. Burk, Jr., was an architect, a classical thinker, a gifted artist, sculptor, and stone carver. He worked in the Los Angeles studio of the noted sculptor Robert Merrell Gage who became his friend and mentor. There they created scores of monumental stone carvings and castings that adorn many of the classical California buildings built in the 1920s and 30s. One will find many of their pediments, fountains and *friezes* on the campus at the University of Southern California.

The depression doomed the Gage's studio business and my parents came to Santa Fe in 1934. Dad, still the artist, was now a practicing architect with a concurrent job as a gas station attendant. With the backing of my mother's father, my parents hand-built an adobe home in which they lived and later sold to facilitate their move to Albuquerque. Dad taught art and architecture at the University of New Mexico and soon became head of the fledgling architecture department. He was the thirty-fourth registered architect in the State of New Mexico. When World War II arrived, his talents became assets for the Manhattan Project as he designed the covert hangars and runways in Alamogordo, New Mexico.

I arrived in 1947. My early memories are of a home filled with art, creative activities and music. My older brother Bill and I were both encouraged from a young age to be creative and to make things with our hands. We were frequently exposed to the performing arts and museums, and I have clear memories of Dad playing piano, painting watercolors and creating portrait busts in clay.

My mother, Suzanne was the kind of person who drew others in with her tremendous humor, kind nature and innate wisdom. When friends arrived at the house, she was always included. A reader, writer and astute grammarian, the breadth of her literacy always amazed me. She frequently engaged us in word games like Tom Swifties, where a funny pun would turn an adverb into a punch line: "I saw her come down the stairs," said Tom condescendingly! My mother instilled in me a love for this kind of banter and words at play—quick quips are a specialty of mine to this day.

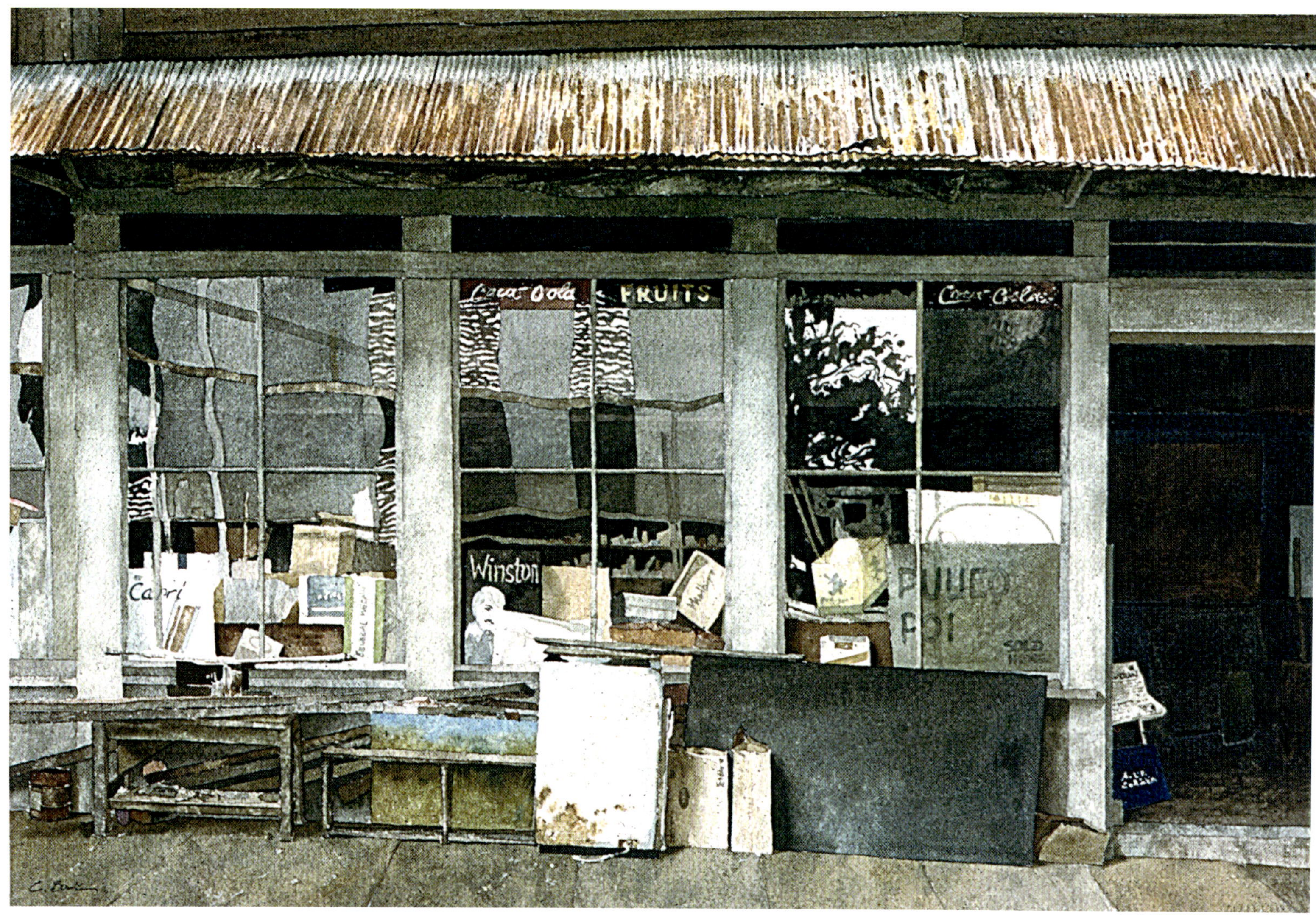

I spent my teen years working in Dad's office as a junior draftsman believing that becoming an architect was my chosen career. I recall being influenced by a charismatic officemate who was an artist and *raconteur*. He was a free spirit, living on the edge of any personal responsibility. At my immature age, I saw his lifestyle as quite seductive. The pull away from the disciplines of architecture had begun.

In 1965 the Vietnam War was raging, and I had begun my studies at the University of New Mexico. Having found the architecture curriculum uninspiring and my draft notice inevitable, I joined the Navy Reserves in 1966. I was fortunate to be assigned to a submarine tender in San Diego Harbor, and later managed to earn a position on shore at the base newspaper as both a journalist and photographer.

Store Front, 1981   15 x 22   Watercolor
 Private Collection

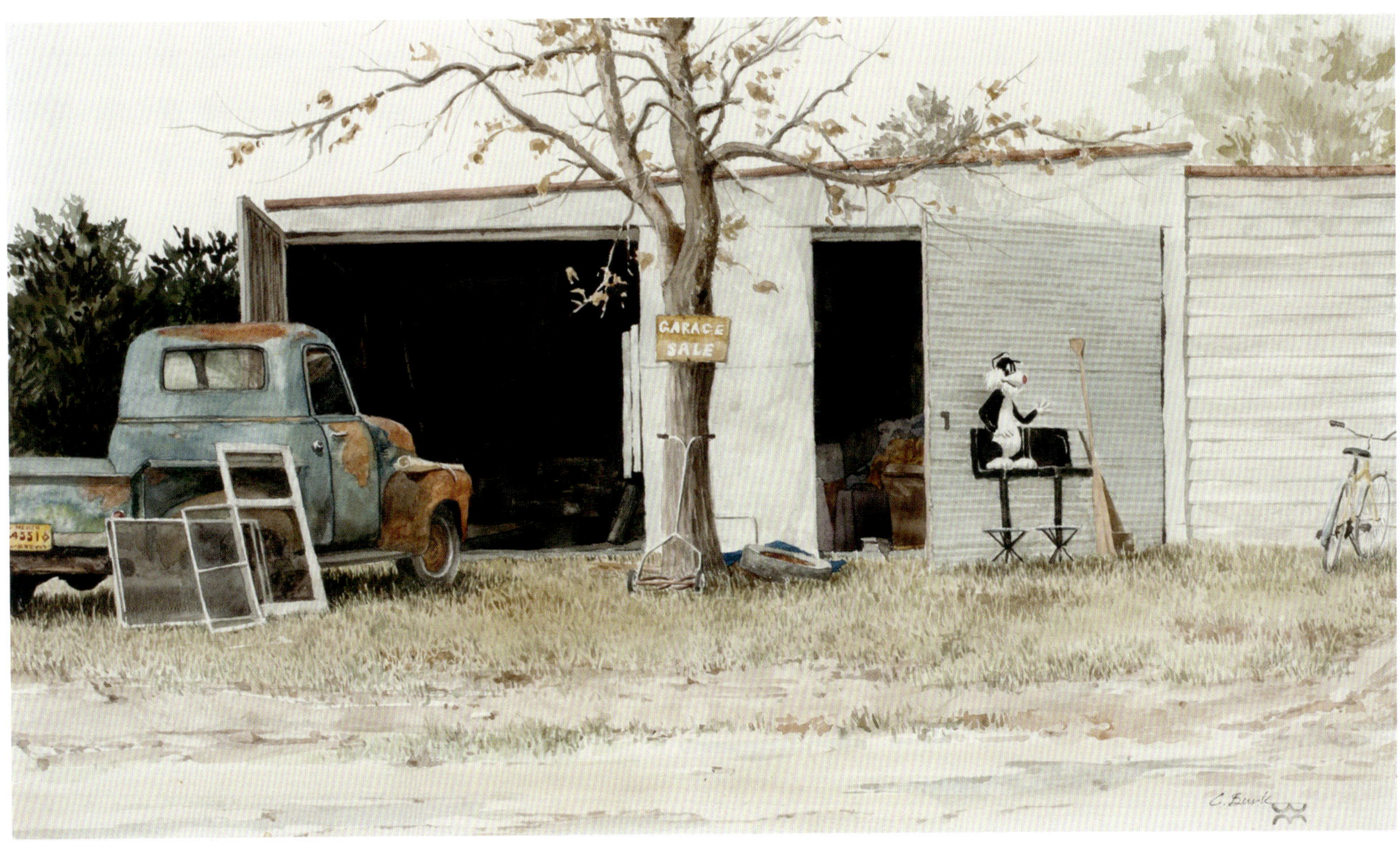

After completion of my service, and now committed to learning all aspects of formal art training, I re-enrolled at the University of New Mexico in 1971 as a fine art major. Conceptual art was the mainstream ideology for most of the 70s. There was enormous pressure on us to have profundity in our work, and to justify our creations with intellectual arguments. I remember writing detailed analyses of minimal art: steel squares on the floor, a blue string in the woods. This intense exercise in critical thinking was highly valued by the professors, at least as much as was the actual execution of our paintings. This discipline stifled bits of my youthful exuberance that was and is my natural nature.

For several years during and after college, I attended organized art fairs and expos and considered this crucial on-the-job training. Traveling to venues in other cities and states was welcome relief, and the art fairs generated some income and offered introductions to my first galleries.

Afternoon Subsequent to a Modest Success, 1983   11½ x 19   Watercolor
Collection of the Artist

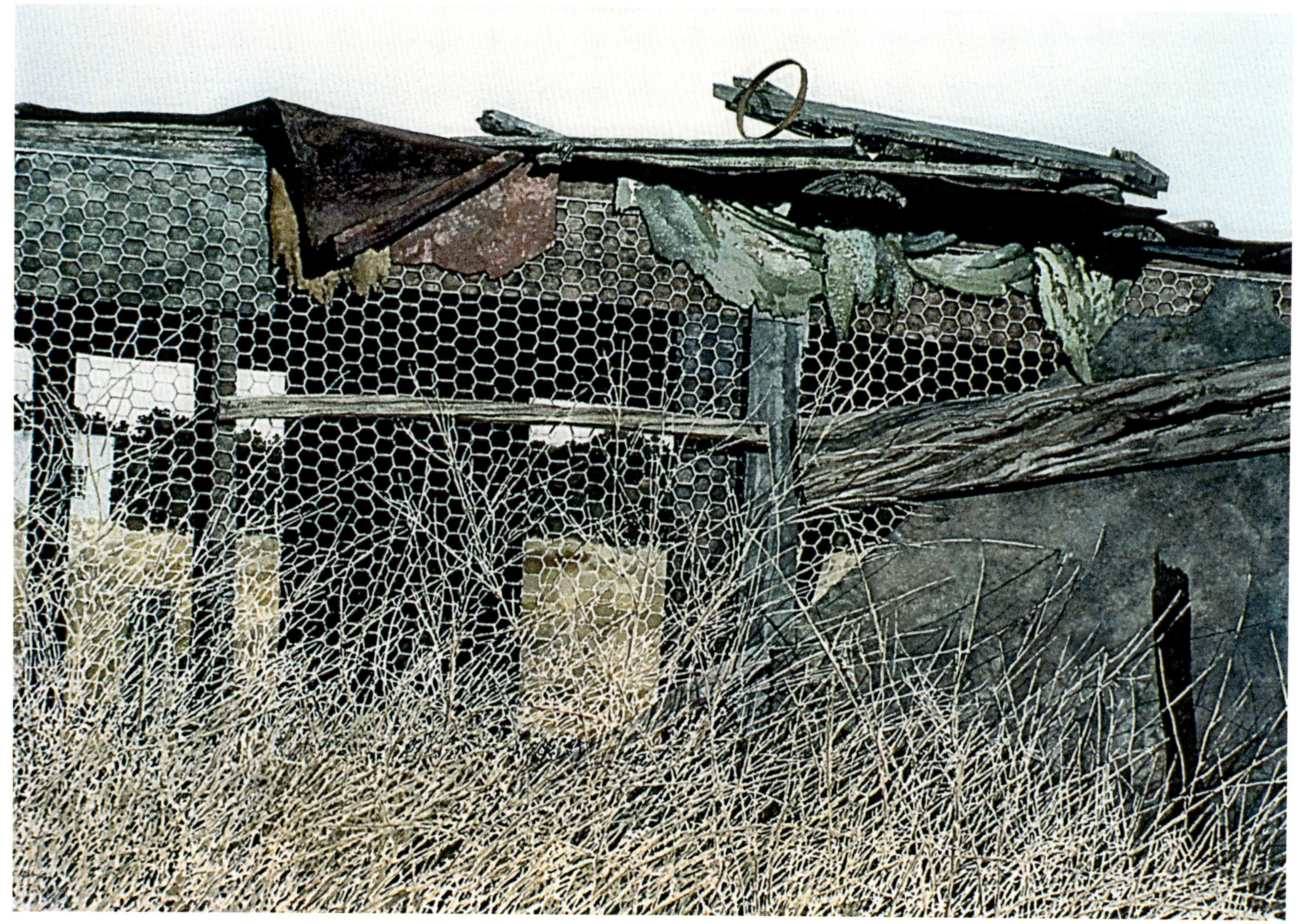

I was awarded a commission in the early 1970s to create 72 paintings for the States Steamship Company. Each of the four new steamships was to be named after an individual state: the Maine, Nevada, Illinois, and Arizona. I was hosted travel to each state to acquire the "feel" of each locale, and to paint images that reflected its uniqueness. I relished the travel and exploration, and eighteen resulting watercolors were hung in the staterooms aboard the four ships. This project helped launch my career and was a sustaining income for two years.

For the next several years, I continued to paint and explore my vision, mostly in watercolor. Working from both photographs and memory, it was the relationship between objects, the betwixt and between, that fascinated me, rather than the actual objects themselves. I sought to challenge reality and to create intrigue using layering, shadows, and the surface of an image to breathe vitality into each piece.

Wood and Wire, 1985   20 x 30   Watercolor

   Collection of Ann and Dick Stables

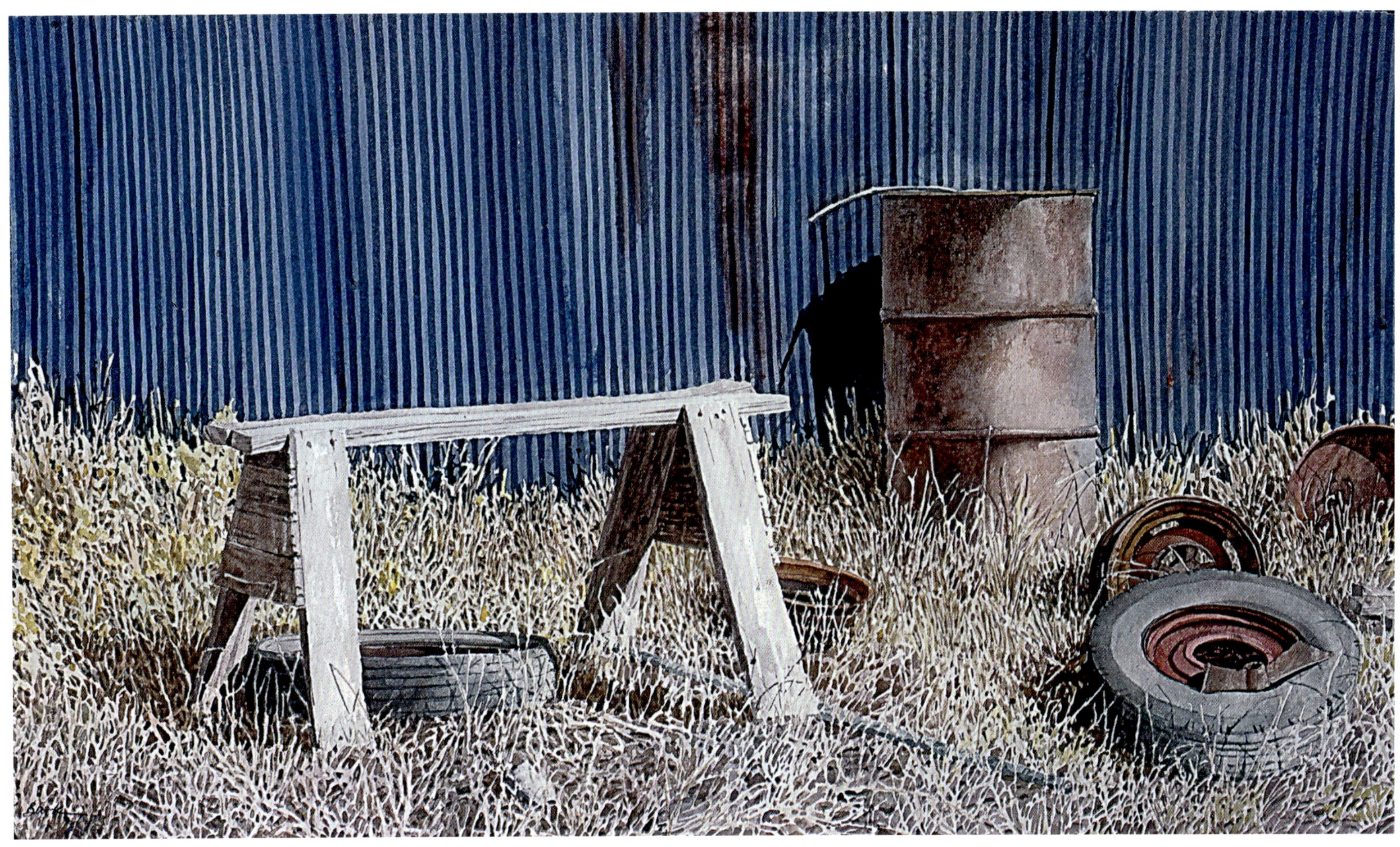

My subjects were objects of the human world juxtaposed with the natural world. Readily available, I would just happen upon them. An old store window with its alluring reflections in the glass would appear. I'd discover a culvert on a walk, chicken wire, natural plants, grasses, a garage sale the day after—those odd final remnants. Many people overlook the ordinary, but I was painting the mundane to give it life. I wanted to illustrate something implied, to make it as compelling in paint as it was in my psyche.

As I painted in watercolor, the nature of the medium offered its own kind of light, one that would shimmer and glow from within. It was a marvelous discovery and inspired me to have my paintings appear to be more than careful depictions of places or objects. The goal was to achieve the "super real," to provide a challenge for people's observations.

Saw Horse, Barrel and Tires, 1985   15 x 22   Watercolor
Private Collection

As I endeavored to create realism with a twist, I was inspired by the artist Jamie Wyeth and his unusual painting style and subject matter. Certainly I was impressed by the 1950s breakthrough work of abstract expressionists like Franz Kline and Robert Motherwell, but I couldn't find myself there. Wyeth, a cohort of the Pop Art movement, was never afraid to create a provocative image or use unusual perspectives. I admired the way he reinvented himself in his pumpkin head painting as much as his iconic portrait of a bale of hay. He underscored that realism can always have more to it.

In the late 80s, the wild ups and downs of the financial market caused several galleries representing my work to close. An artist friend, Pat Harrison, had a contract to paint murals at Intel Corporation in Albuquerque and asked me to join in that effort. We began a partnership, grew the business together, and over the course of ten years went on to create over sixty murals at Intel. Other mural locations were Presbyterian Hospital, PNM Electric, private homes, restaurants, businesses, and even one at a challenging highway underpass! I enjoyed it tremendously and was pleased to have new subject matter presented to me. This entire experience helped me grow. In 1998, we each decided it was time to retire the business and return exclusively to studio painting and exhibiting in fine art galleries.

The transition to painting in oil was a natural progression from the acrylic paints we used in creating murals. I wonder now why it took so long to realize the advantages. Painting from light to dark in watercolor necessitated a tedious process that I trained myself to enjoy. In fact, I revelled in it. The technique gave the paintings greater importance because of the difficulty and effort required in their creation. I soon realized I could paint with as much complexity as I wanted to in oil. New freedoms in oil techniques offered larger formats, an ease of layering, color mixing, and brought liberation and spontaneity to my work. Painting became like a weaving, in and out, through and back again, translating what I was viewing into something uniquely mine. I was entranced by surface abstraction, not focused on a particular scene. My fascination with grasses as a subject intensified and I felt at home. I wanted my form of realism to provoke, to have viewers say, "Whoa, what is *that*?" Perhaps they would look again, and leave with unanswered questions.

I have been determined to do what I love; it has not been an easy path. My journey was supplemented with a variety of labors and adventures for many of the early years. Creating art is such a personal expression—the highs and lows can be profoundly impactful. It takes persistence and experience to maintain momentum and to gain confidence. In addition to what I see, I wish a journey into imagination for all who witness my work.

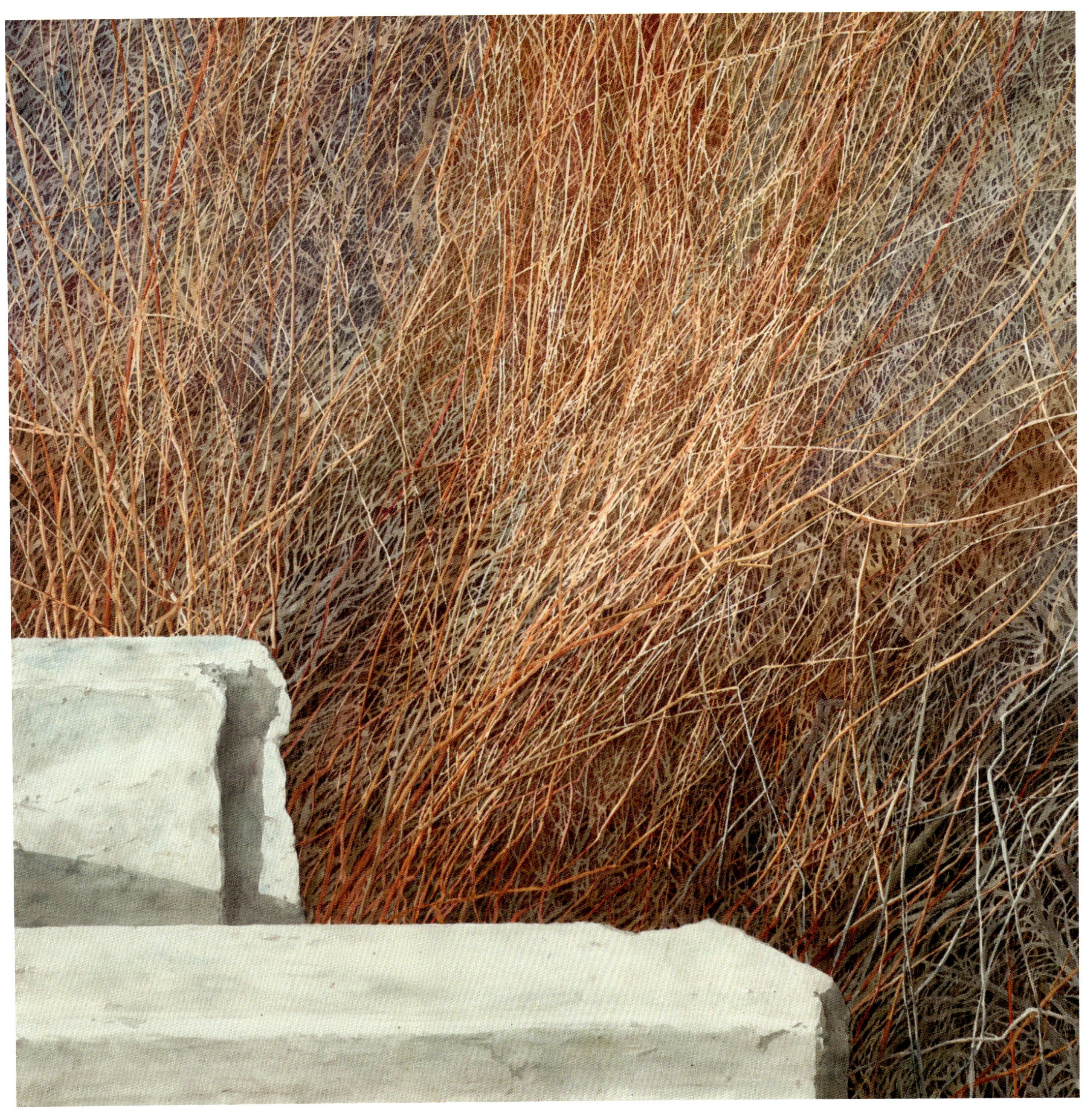

Square Entry, 1990   40 x 40   Watercolor
Collection of the Artist   17

"I nurture a conceptual approach to realism by exploring abstraction, and rejecting sentimentalism. Watercolors must be painted light to dark because it is a transparent medium. The lighter shapes must be painted first. Painting many layers of receding lines creates a faceted effect. Every dip of the brush varies slightly in value. The subject grows in depth and detail behind the forward surface. Much of the art is viewed "between the lines."

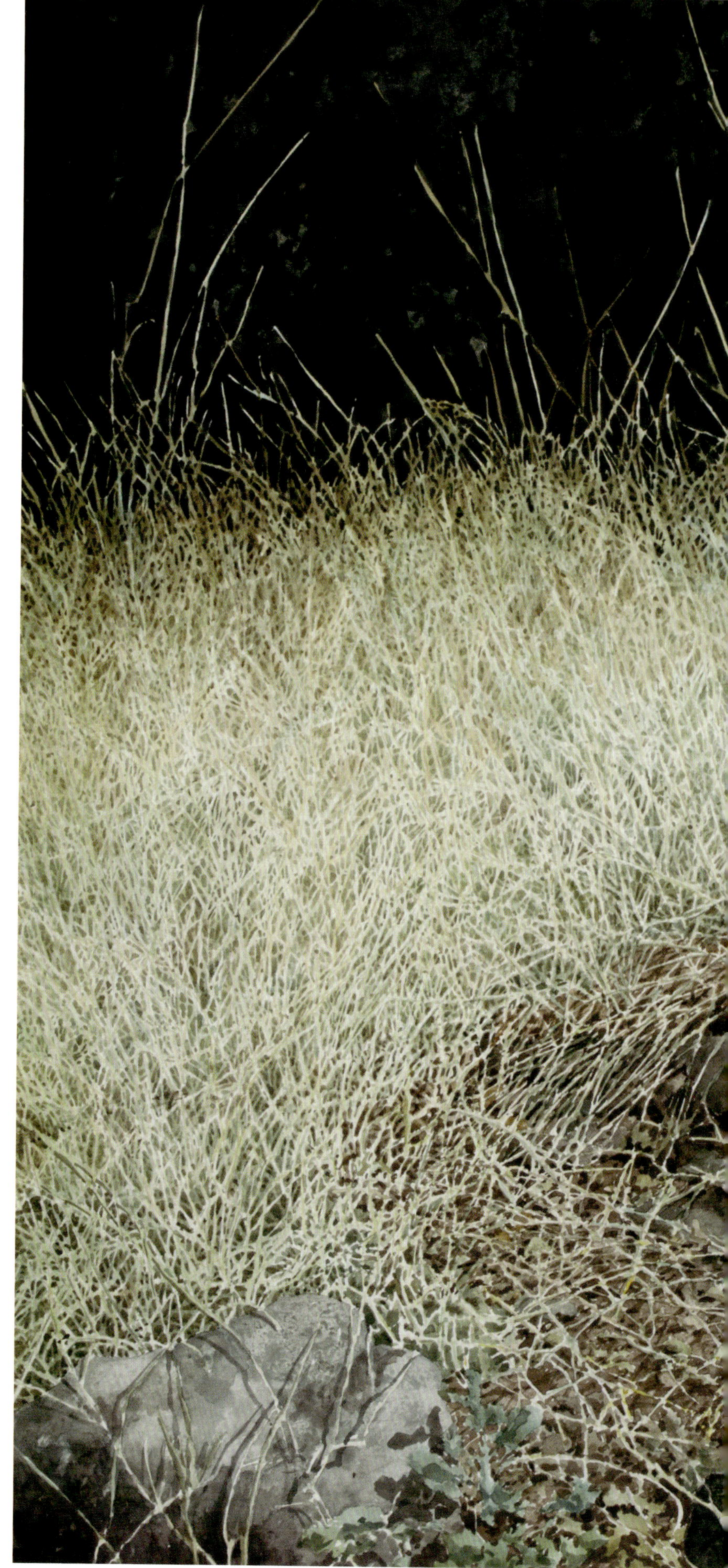

Site of an Unattended Montana Picnic, 1992   22½ x 35   Watercolor
Collection of Jinni and Dave Thomas

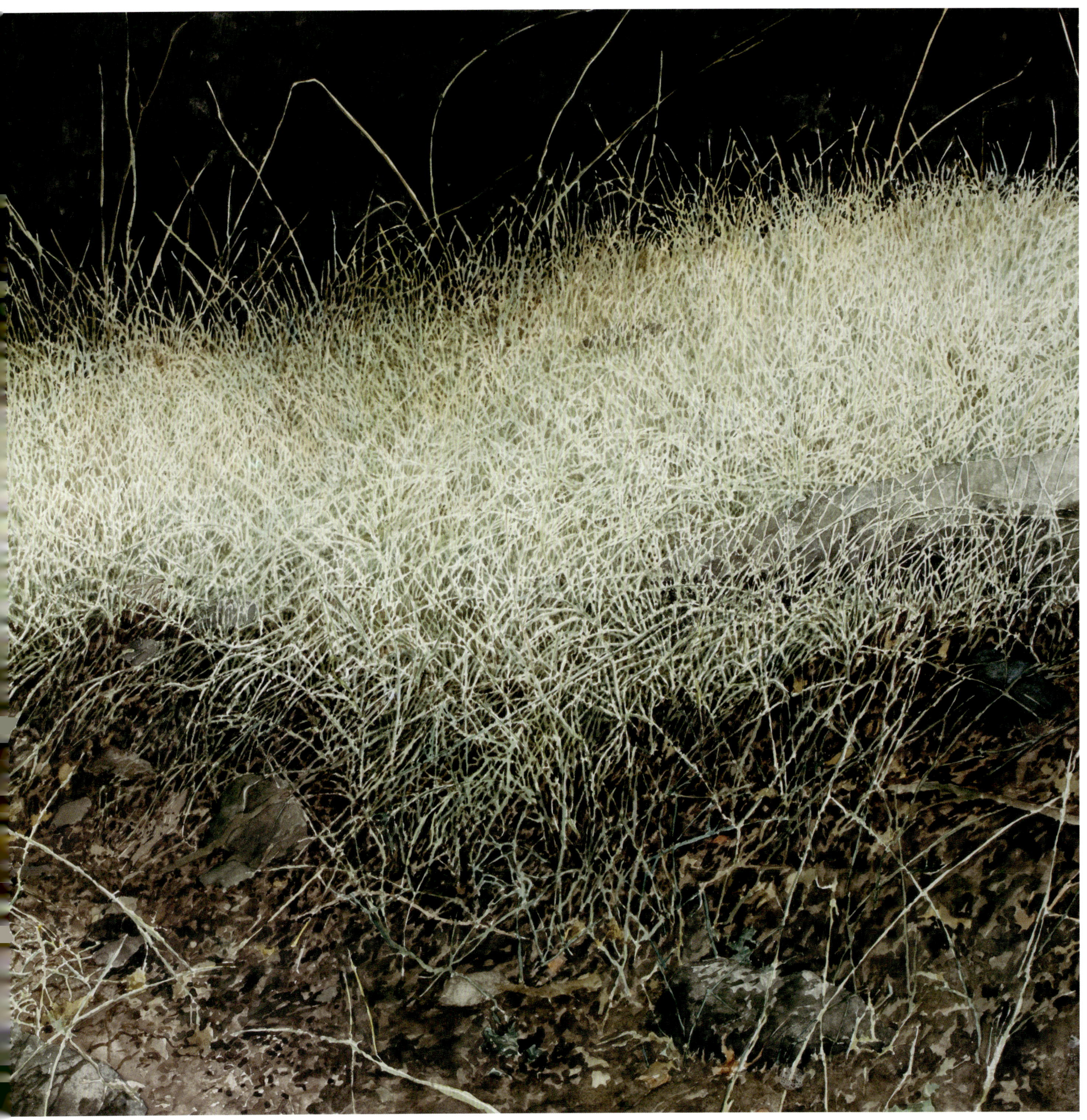

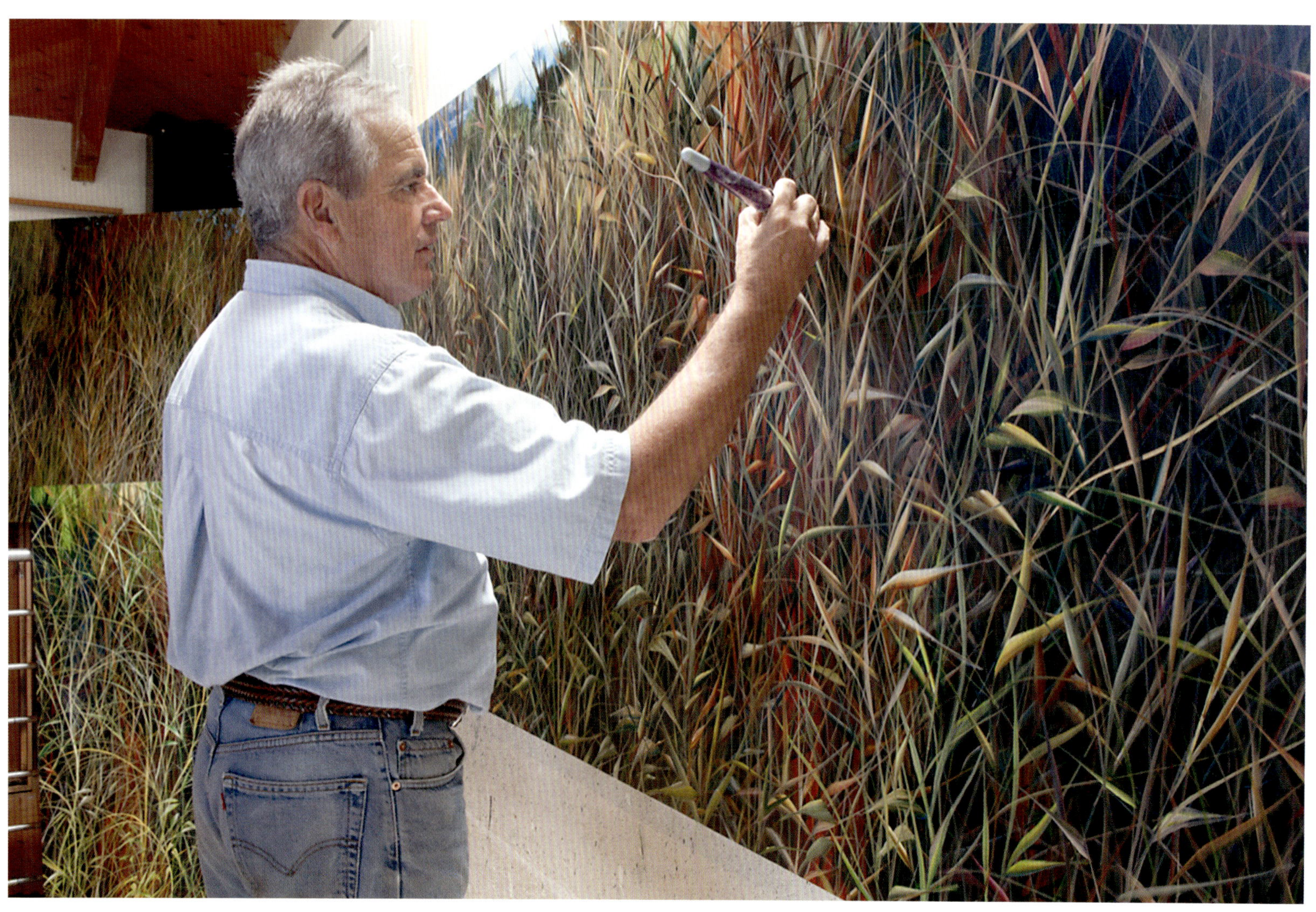

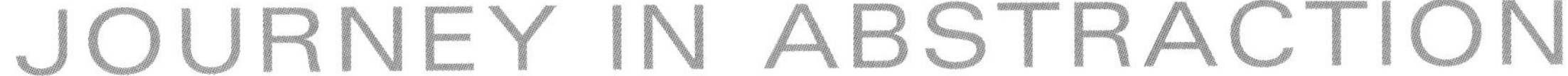

JOURNEY IN ABSTRACTION

"In 1999, I left watercolors behind and began painting in oil. I could paint the same obsessive detail, and found it much easier to paint dark to light than light to dark. I was no longer limited by size. The oil paint-ing offered spontaneity not available in watercolor painting. Untitled 1 was created in response to an art gallery invitation. Painting the grass texture in oil was a welcomed departure. It liberated my mind to quickly shift further into the abstraction I longed to explore. The art moved beyond realism into a new unexplored territory. This was the start of a new series, and an extraordinary partnership began."

Untitled I, 2004   48 x 48   Oil on panel

     Collection of Ginni Brown

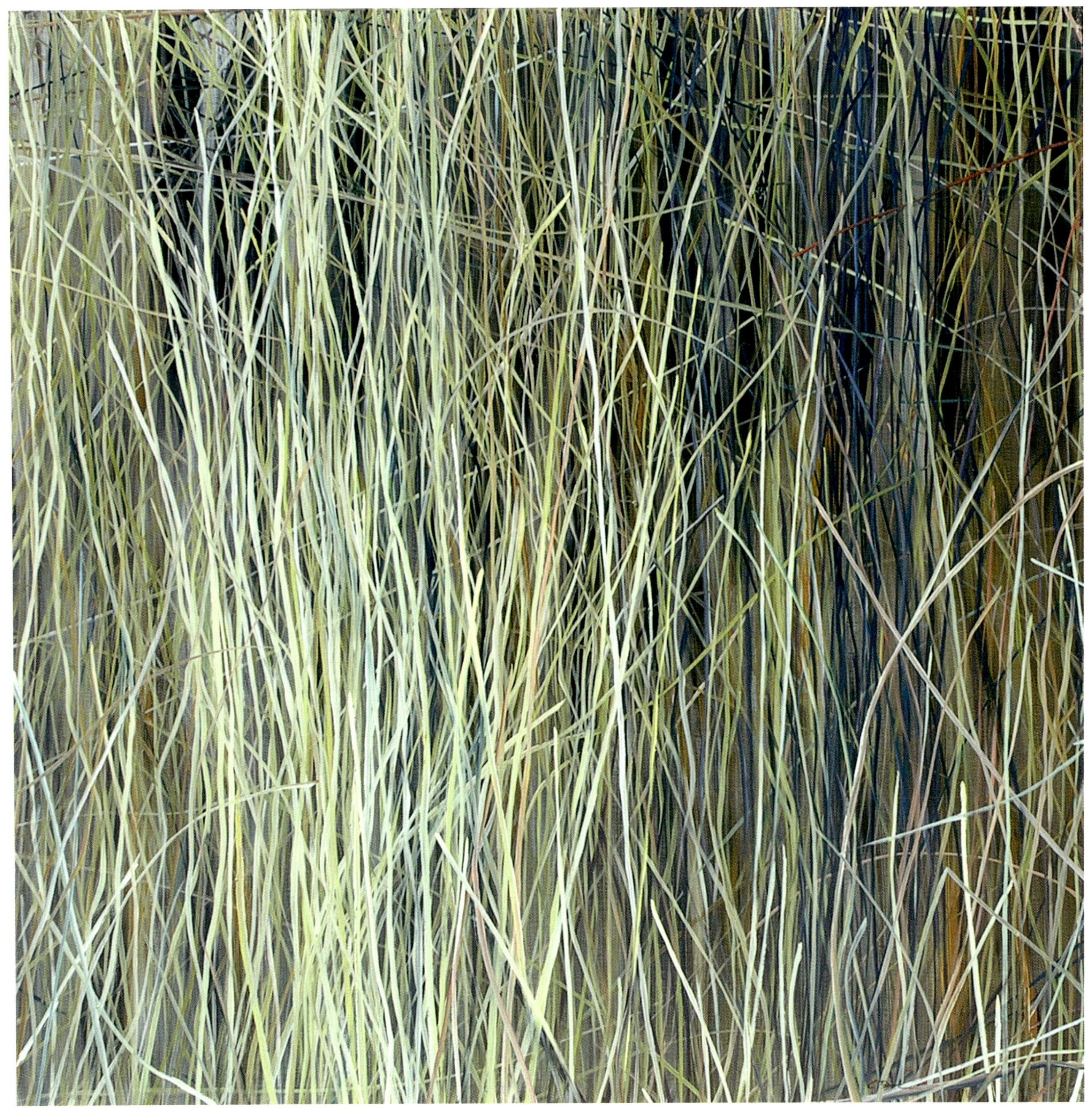

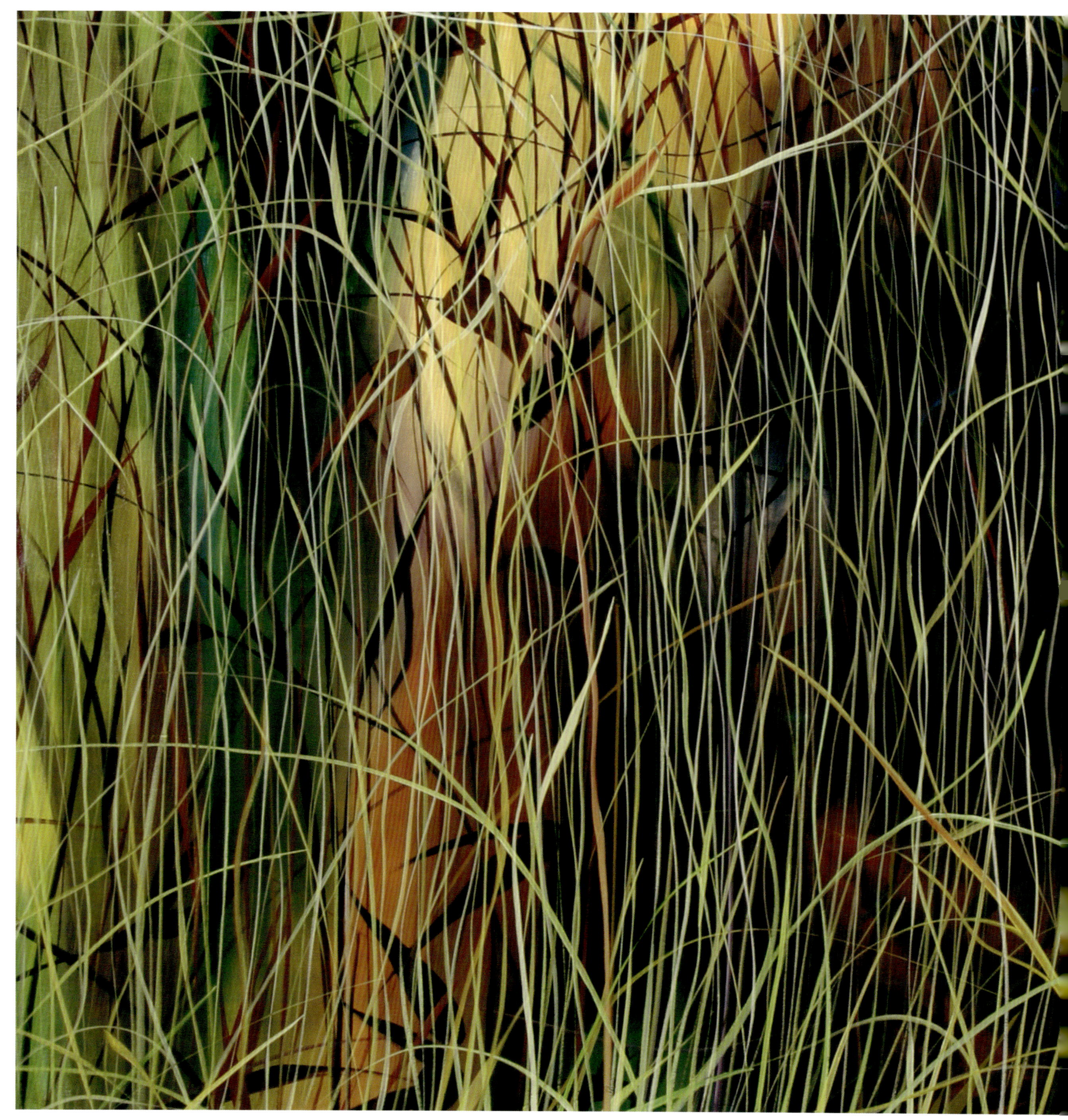

Untitled XXXXV, 2005   48 x 96   Oil on panel

    Collection of Maggy and David Croxville

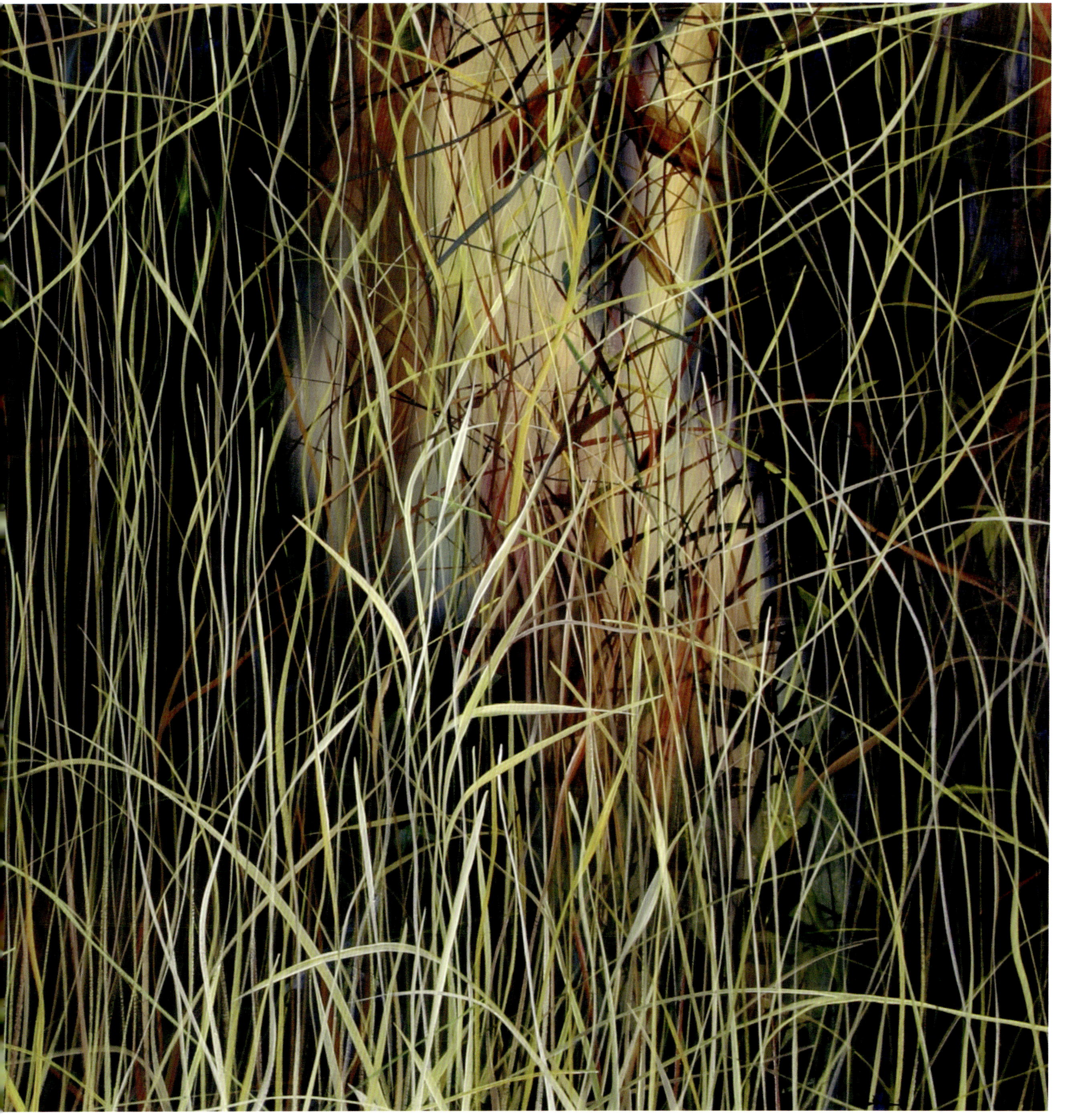

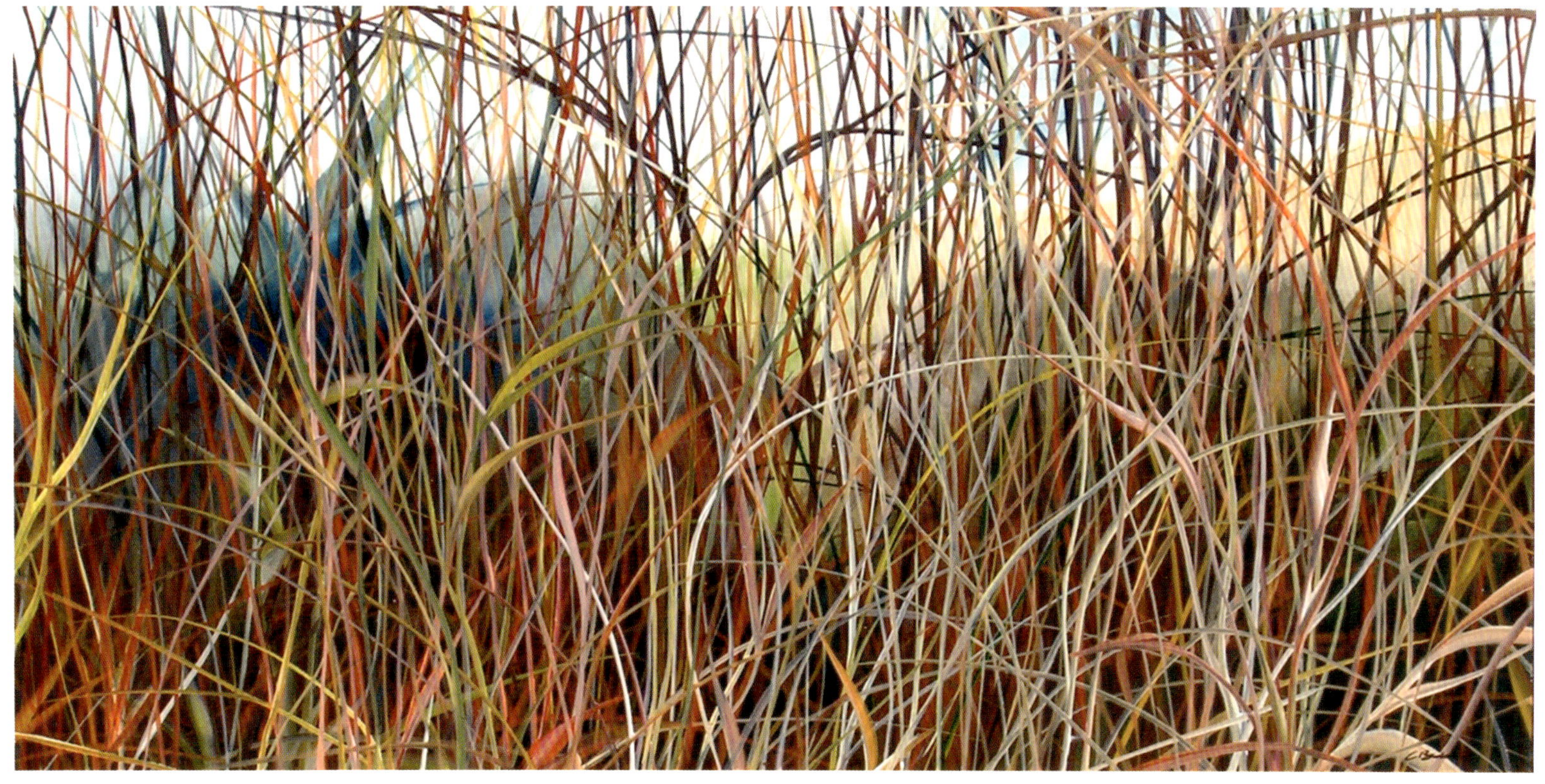

Untitled No. 83, 2006   24 x 48   Oil on panel

  Collection of Jan and David Friedlander

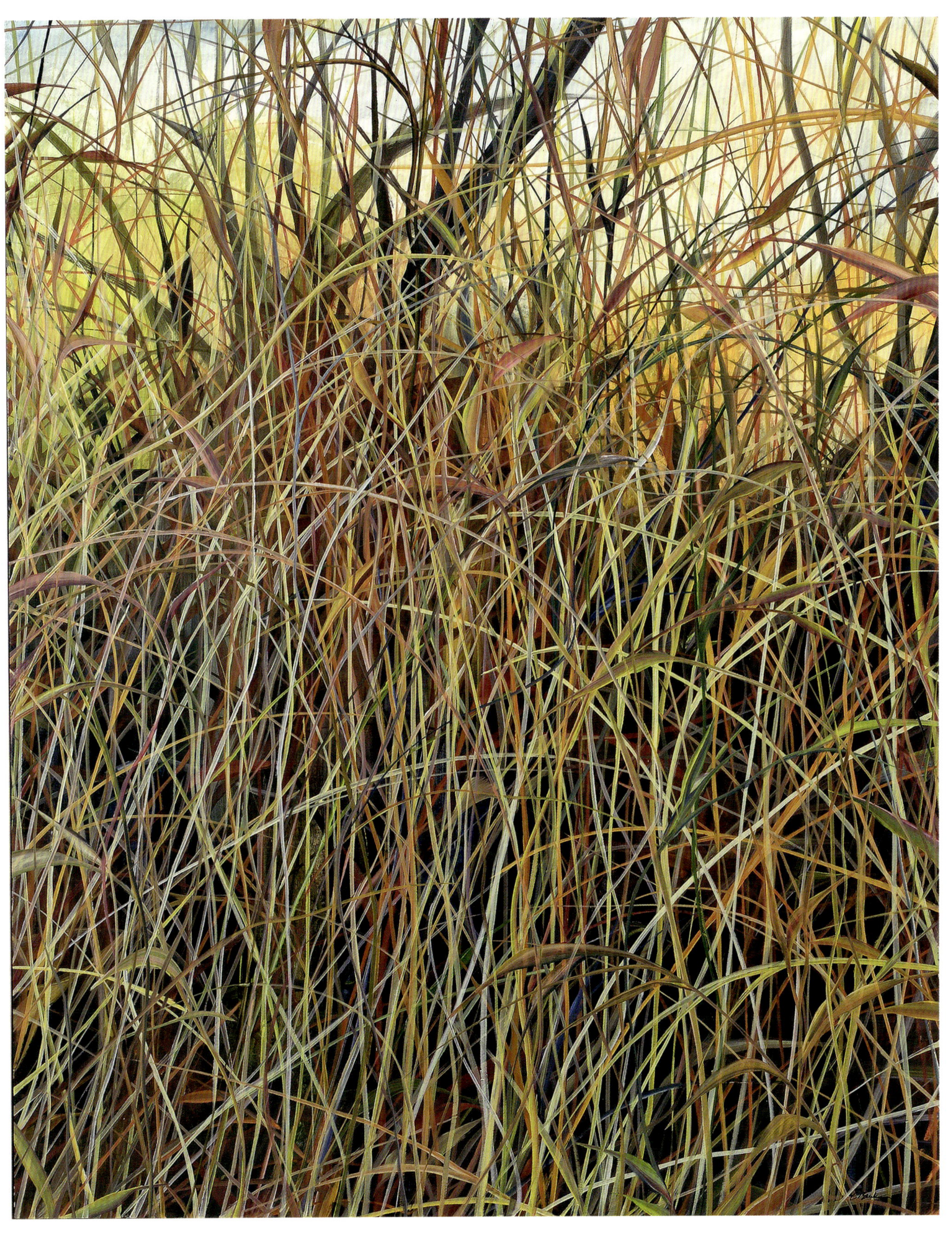

Warm Afternoon, 2006   60 x 48   Oil on panel
Collection of Paula and Ken Weissman

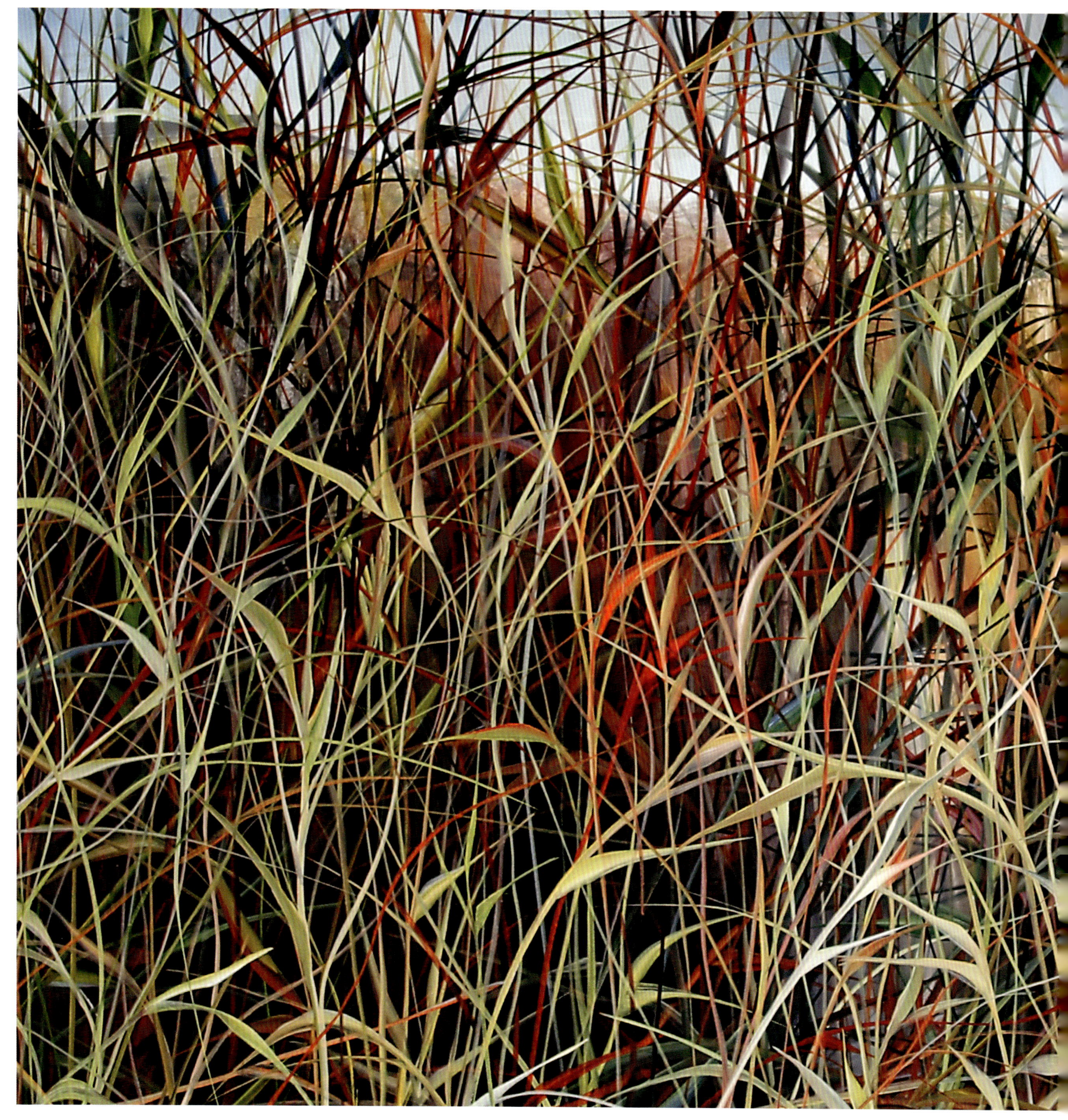

Summer Jazz, 2007   48 x 96   Oil on panel

    Private Collection

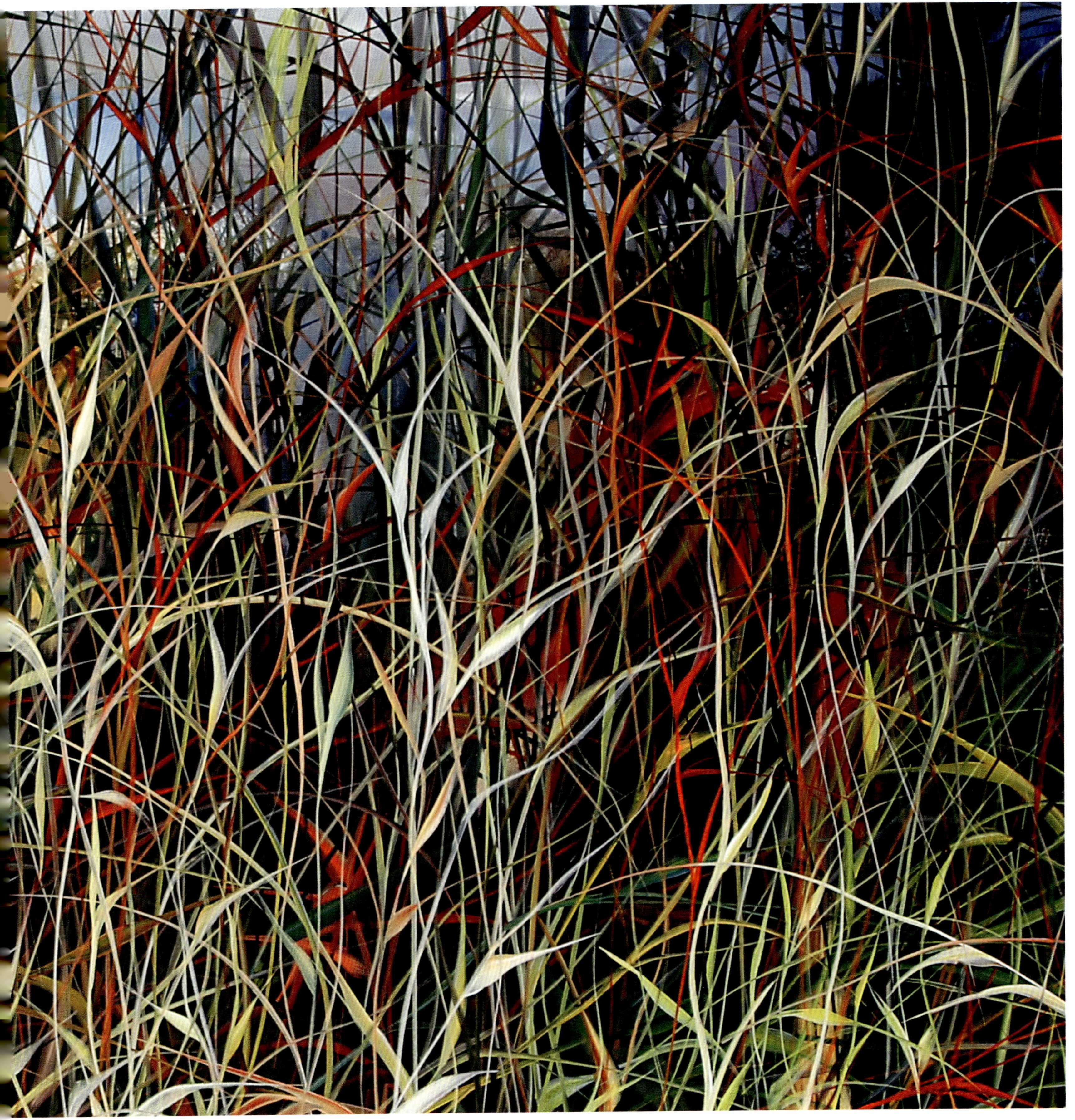

STILLNESS IN THE GRASS

CLAUDIA JOSEPH

There is something elusive yet calming in Charlie Burk's series of grasses fashioned in oil on panel. They thoughtfully and seductively pull the viewer close for a better look, but any conclusions drawn are the observer's alone. Charlie Burk does not set out to create anything remotely identifiable or representational in his work, in fact, he begins without any sort of plan. An abstract image materializes and the artist lives with this newly created canvas for awhile. These early visions then demand to be obscured and filled up with a macro view of grasses, according to Burk.

Looking at these luminous and organic depictions of grass in large format, one is immediately struck by the peacefulness they evoke, likened only to the tranquility one feels from being in Nature. The balance of color and the feeling of a sense of place conspire to make one feel as though they have just plopped down in a field of grass teeming with possibility. But when I prod Charlie Burk about his inspiration for these seeming odes to Mother Nature I wait to hear about his connectedness to the Earth and its many marvels. I continue to wait. This is not to say that Burk does not draw on Nature to execute his work, clearly it is informed by this source. However, the true revelation is that these vertical wisps and sinuous tendrils are not necessarily even "grass" in Burk's mind. They are vehicles of abstraction in and of themselves—merely a means of layering paint.

Perhaps the idea of bringing the outdoors in to create environs in unlikely places developed from Burk's early large scale paintings of painstakingly detailed jungle imagery that took many months to create. These enormous works focused on heavy plant life and the wonderful interplay of shadow and light. Through these large scale works Burk perfected such arduous tasks as recreating the action of a drop of dew descending from a leaf. The lessons gleaned from such intricate painting have been translated skillfully into Burk's Grass Series.

When people seek validation of what they believe they have seen in the background of Burk's pieces, the artist is quick to assure them that these works did not evolve as sentimental images. According to Burk, "People relate to these paintings as scenes, although they are not intended to be reminiscent of any real time, place, or thing." Burk favors the intangible nature of such abstract art, which permits the work to be appreciated for how it looks, yet allows space for people to find their own meaning in it.

Charlie Burk is the thinking man's artist. He wants to provoke an intellectual response to his work—hence his abstract leanings. He notes, "Abstraction lends itself to utilizing intellect to identify with a painting, rather than relying solely on an emotional response. If someone doesn't have a visceral reaction to the work then they are forced to think about it in another, less obvious way." He is a big picture thinker himself, appreciating each work in the series only minimally for its individual merit. Instead he prefers the perspective gained when viewing a large body of work, like the Grass Series as a whole, which affords an appreciation of where the work began and where it is going.

As for where this is going, Burk is not done with grasses by a long shot. His body of work in this form continues to ripen; his expression of abstraction through a veil of grass continues to excite him. He is not alone.

Bosque Thicket, 2008   48 x 48   Oil on panel
 Collection of Patricia Lyle and Scott Bailey

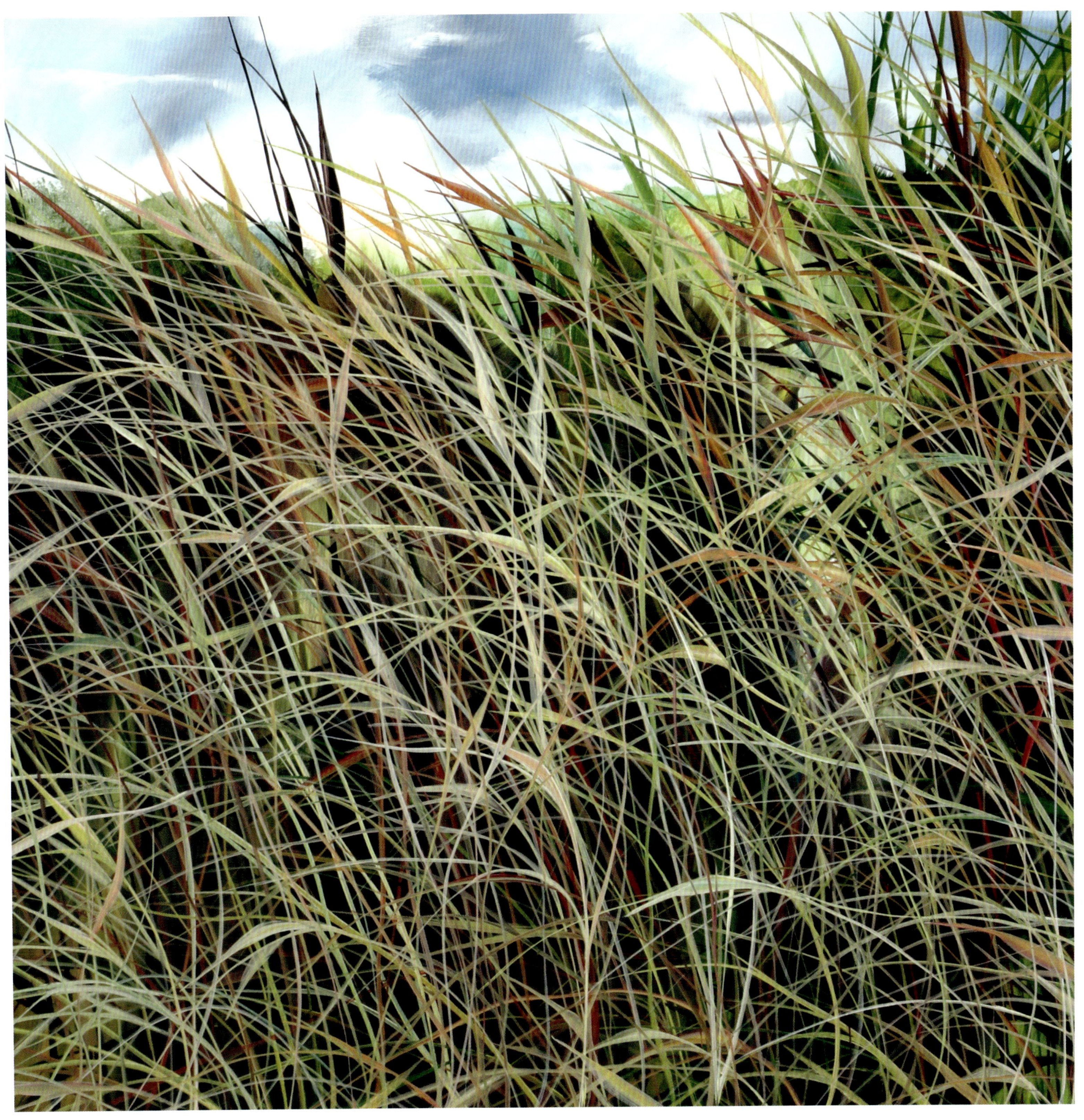

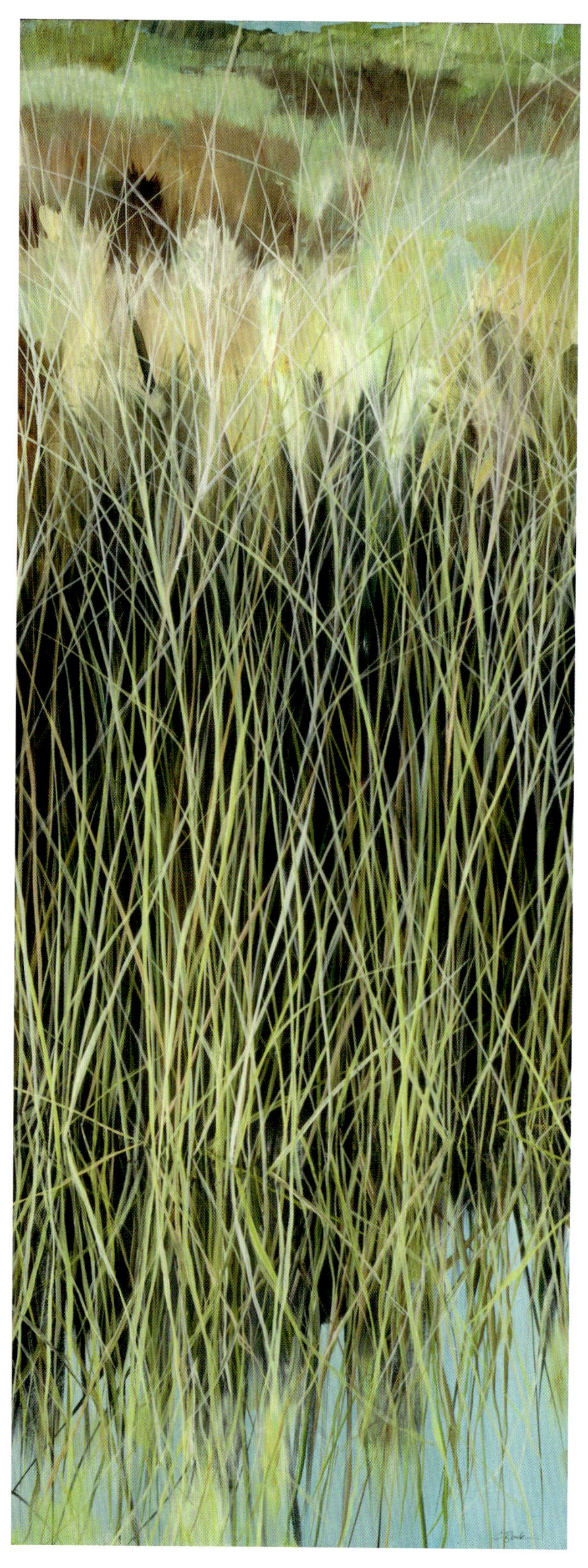

Cool Reflection, 2016   49 x 19   Oil on panel

    Collection of Bonnie Macdonald and Robert Amter

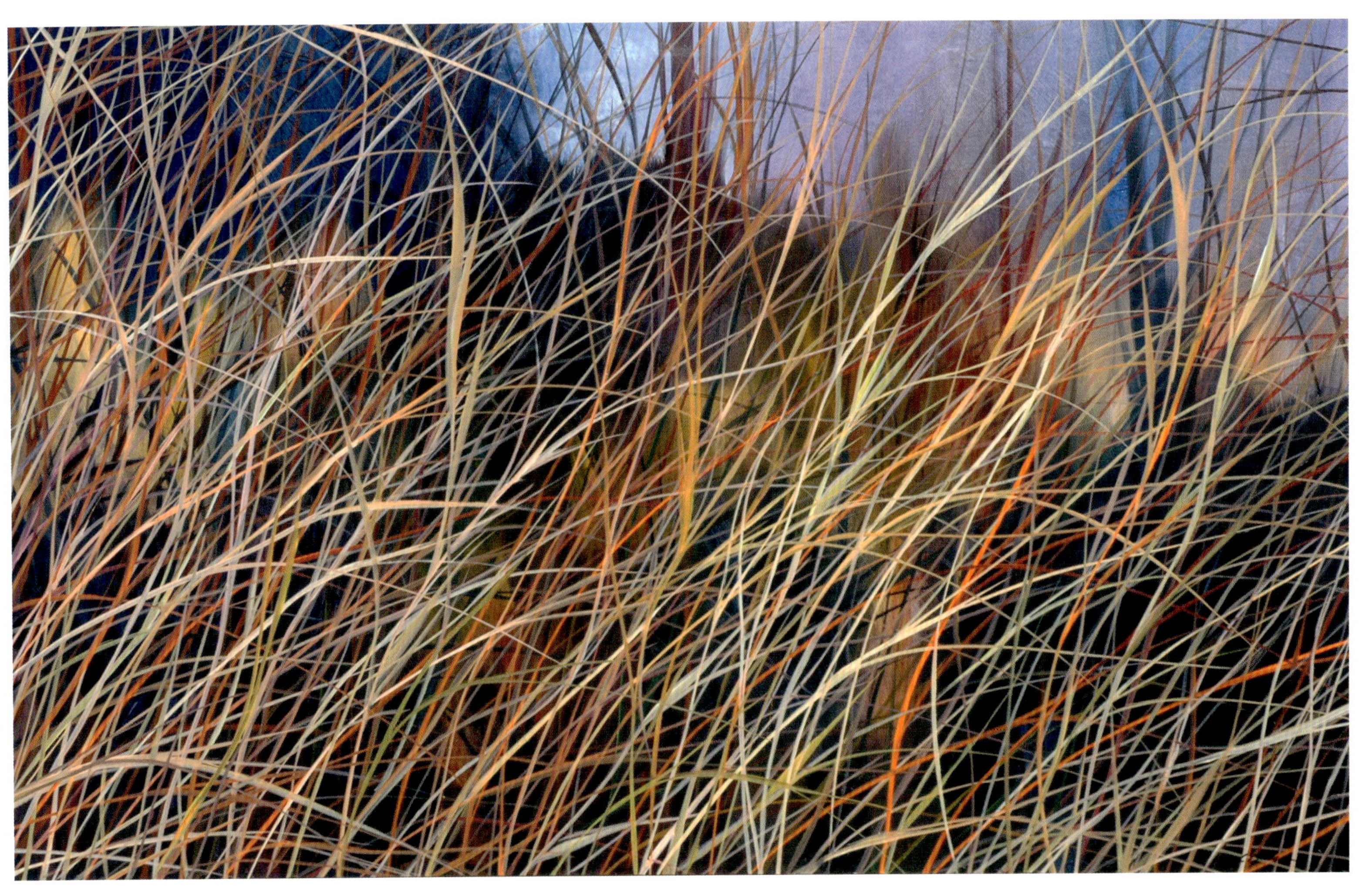

Fireflies, 2009   30 x 48   Oil on panel
Collection of Thomas Ashley   35

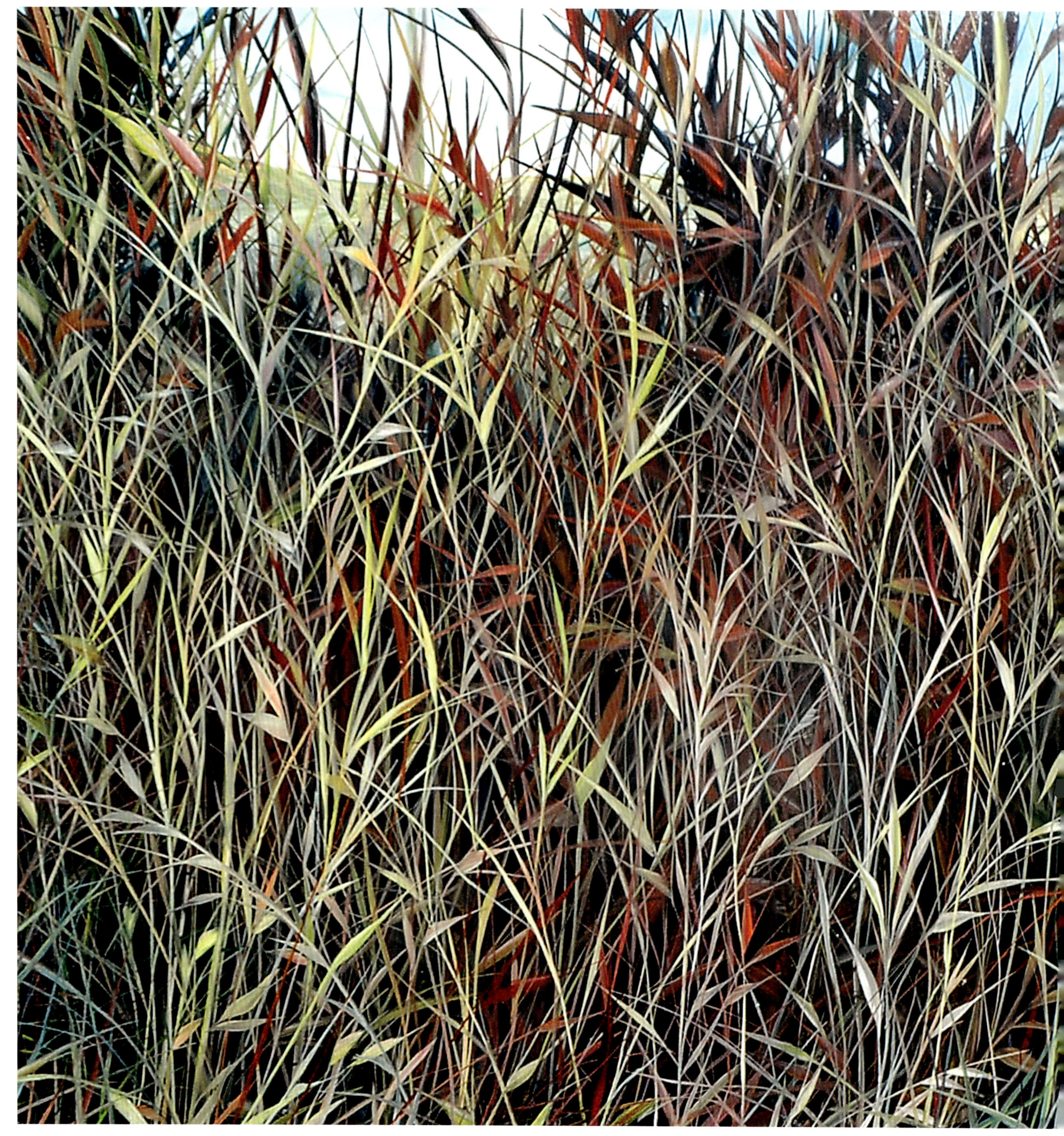

Nature's Glory, 2011   48 x 96   Oil on panel

    Collection of Wendy and Andrew Bivins

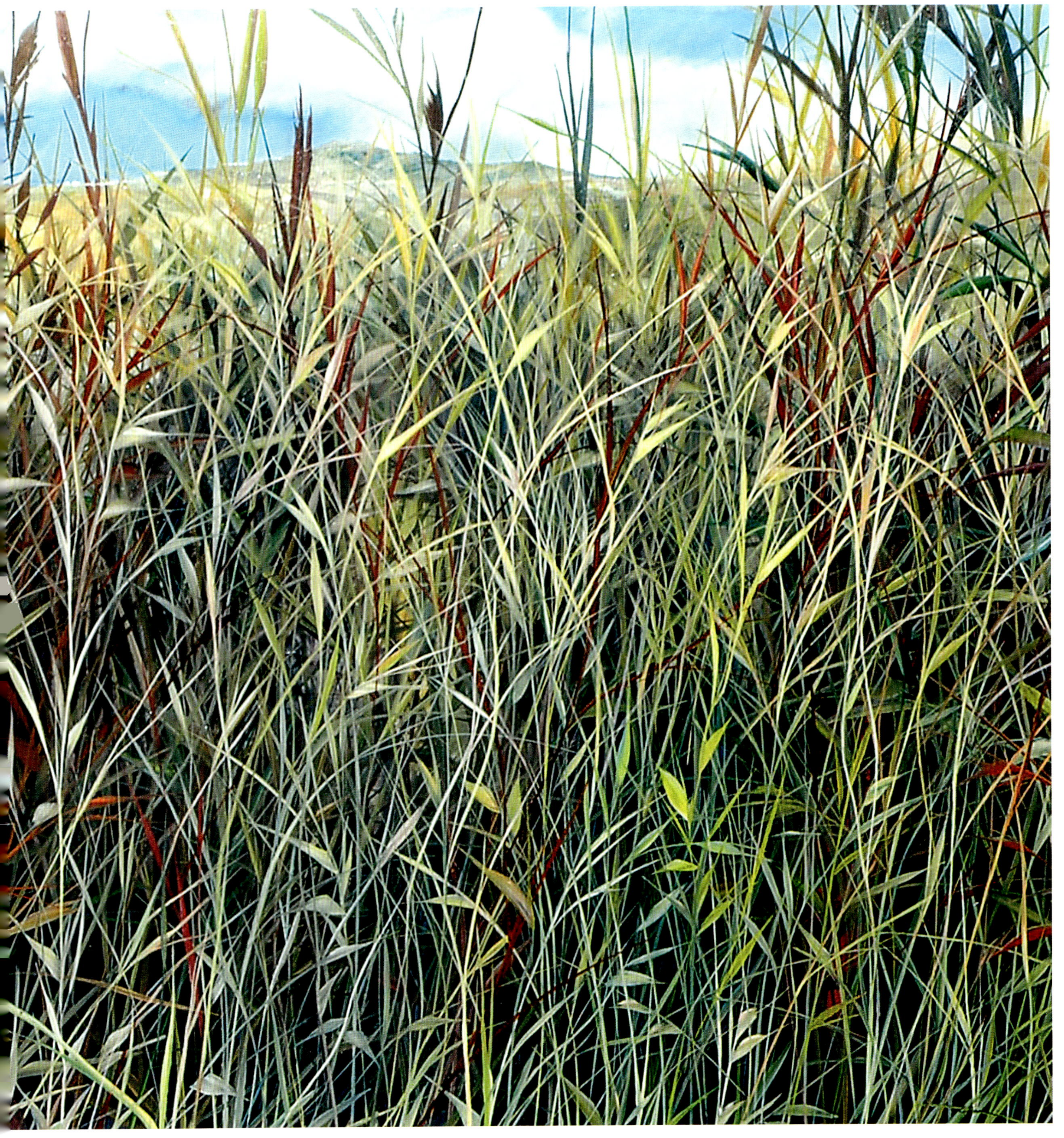

"This painting grew out of my interest in creating a monochromatic work of art within a limited color pallete. I begin each work by creating a flat, textured surface, responding to brushstroke upon brushstroke. The process is reactive—building the image by continuing to add and redact until the painting asks for nothing more."

Grace I, 2009   42 x 42   Oil on panel

 Collection of Louise Rorer Rosett and Walter Rosett

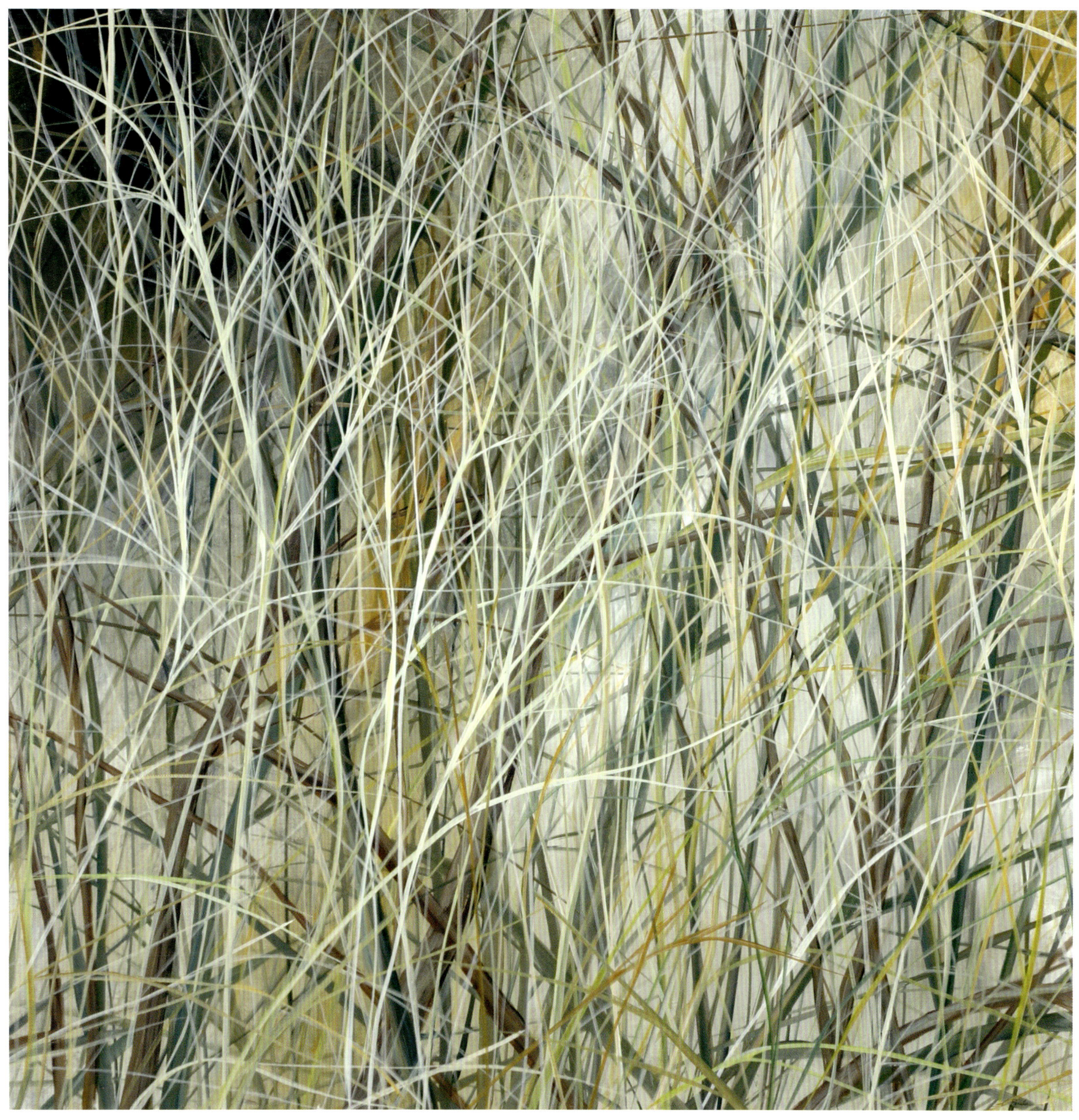

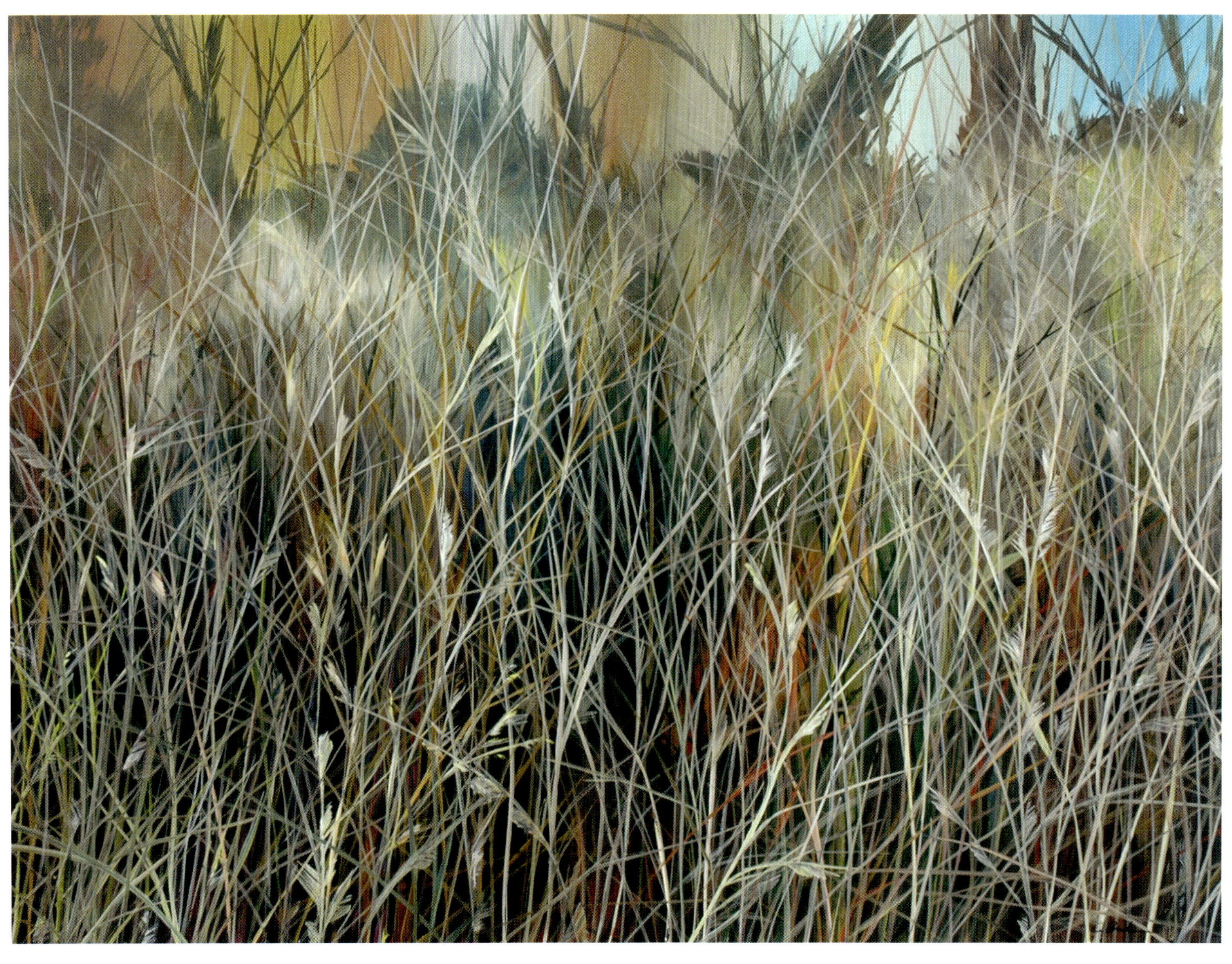

Morning Glow, 2013   30 x 40   Oil on panel

    Collection of Debra S. Nolan

SPRING FORTH

IRIS MCLISTER

"When one tugs at a single thing in nature, he finds it attached to the rest of the world."

—John Muir

In order to understand something large, we isolate and examine its details. This rather simple concept is one that effloresces with virtuosic color and stunning clarity in the paintings of Charlie Burk. A lifelong resident of New Mexico, Burk departs from contemporary art's increasingly conceptual protocols with his depictions of light-saturated thickets of grass and sky that bear witness to the earth's abundant, simple beauty. Nature is Burk's consort and constant, and grass, arguably Nature's most humble and everyday feature, is his main visual objective. Close-cropped, ground-level perspectives focus our attention on vignettes, not panoramas, of landscape. In limiting our perspective, Burk imbues small sections of earth with resounding significance. This sort of pictorial distillation manifests in meticulously conceived paintings that are almost obsessive in their desire to reproduce the untrammeled and effortless harmony of wilderness settings. Burk's lush, crisply realistic depictions of grassy vistas advocate a distinctly unusual hierarchy of genres, wherein Nature's humble ground floor is assigned top compositional billing. From this intimate perspective, the earth's subtle rhythms occur as both vast and bracingly proximate.

Grasses grow dense, springing forth from unseen soil. They are both faithfully rendered and decidedly painterly, espousing the simple and hearty beauty of the outdoors—crucial sustenance for those of us whose urban lives can too often leave us feeling estranged from Nature. Burk conveys a contagious reverence for his humble subject. In *Morning Glow*, a pervasive mist is fuzzily nestled amongst the vegetation. The feathery, blooming tops of wild switchgrass and bluestem nevertheless attain compositional supremacy, their wispy, overlapping stalks reflecting Nature's haphazard beauty. Dense foliage is intriguingly set against a sky whose smoky oranges and yellows merge into an abstracted sunset. Burk doesn't punctuate his work with trees or rocks; instead we are encouraged to study specific, nuanced aspects of the natural world.

Burk's subject matter identifies him as a painter of landscapes, a genre whose venerable forbears notably include Hudson River School painters Thomas Cole, Fredric Edwin Church, and Thomas Moran, among many others: artists with a collectively ambitious approach to the great outdoors. On canvas, this engagement translated into sprawling paintings, rife with drama and romance, often spread across correspondingly large surfaces. Intentionally or otherwise, these epic vistas were designed to capture earth's vastness at a time when photography was either nonexistent or in its infancy. Working in times when photography is ubiquitous, it is remarkable that Burk so utterly achieves a similarly transportive ability. Nevertheless, his carefully chosen, tautly focused vantages are steadfastly modern in outlook and affect.

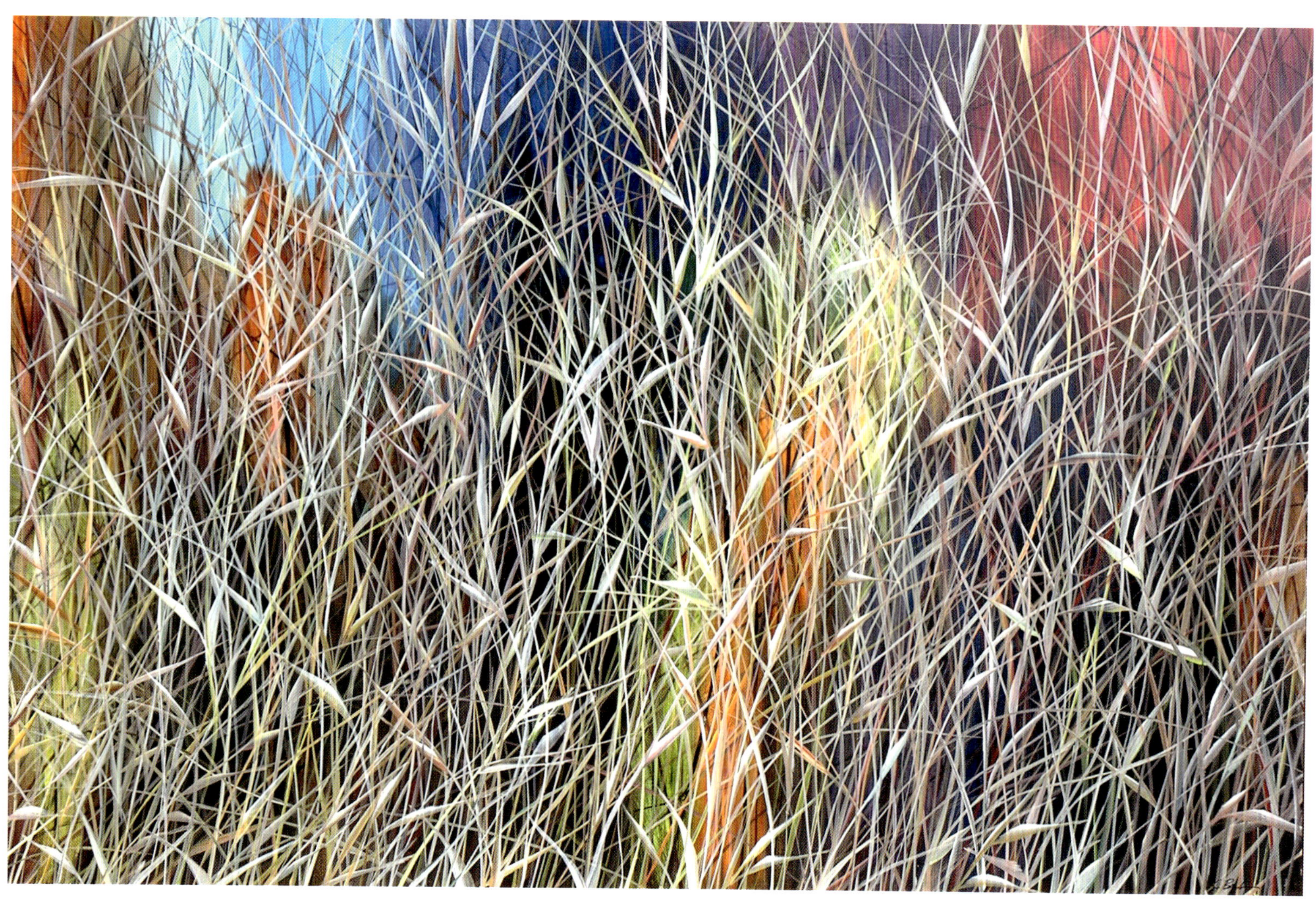

Lyric Afternoon, 2015   32 x 49   Oil on panel

  Collection of Gayle and Lonny Siegel

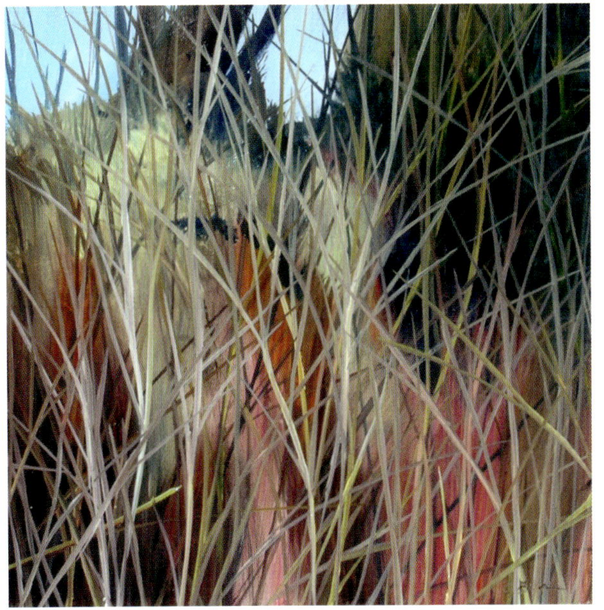

Ribbon-like blades of dappled grass ripple and recede into a cloudy, rainbow-hued sky in *Lyric Afternoon*. A marvelous tension is created in this dichotomy of the pale, cool outer layer of tangled stalks set against the darkening, abstracted sky. Showcasing riotous color and painterly brushstrokes, Burk's skies are full of abstract impulses. Just beyond his delicately rendered blades of grass are un-resolved dashes and strokes of bold color. This tension is repeated throughout his paintings, which juxtapose elegant restraint with an essential wildness. Untamed as they are, Burk's compositions belie keen foresight. Colors blend imperceptibly into each other or else occur as stridently differentiated, but always they ring of precise order. One's impression is that Burk carefully controls his paintings' direction, calculating the scope and content—and according visual effect—of each composi-tion. Burk's practice depends on the implementation of a wide range of colors, whose values shift from warm to cool many times over within the space of a single composition.

Even when modestly scaled, Burk utilizes every available surface area, an energetic facility affirmed in works like the diminutive *Garden Song*, which measure just a square foot. Thin blades of grass are rendered in easy strokes of dusky mauve and pale green. These bright stalks are interspersed with a jumble of pinks and violets—a *mélange* of color that would be firmly abstract without its overlay of meticulously crafted foliage. Dispatches of turquoise and streaky yellow seem to alchemically merge to form the sky. Of course the viewer's immediate response is one of recognition: here is grass, and beyond it sky—but this initial analysis gives way to a larger sense of expansiveness and possibility.

Burk's compositions feel welcoming—almost lived-in, or just vacated and redolent with humanity, even though they are markedly absent of its *accoutrements*. The frank omission incites our powerful animal attraction to Nature, whose irregular beauty was described by Victorian-era critic and painter John Ruskin as "… conducive to the rest and health of the human frame." The horizontal expanse of *Luxurious Passage* is overlain with arching blades of grass. Light glints across individual stalks, which seem to shimmer and dance before us. In the lower portion of the panel, the blades look tread-upon and flat-tened; perhaps a rare suggestion of human or animal occupation. The top of the painting is dominated by a distant tree line and a multi-colored sky. It is a narrow strip of cerulean blue and creamy white that some-how anchors the grassy foreground, which seems to glimmer and shift as our eyes travel from left to right.

Depending on how a work is lit, as well as the position of the viewer, a single composition contains myriad visual interpretations. Seemingly endless variations of green are joined by a parade of colors that enhance the verdant terrain. Glimpses of crisp yellow, Venetian purple, and crimson share space with dashes of pale violet and burnt sienna, all adorning the wild flora to accentuate Nature's boundless, kaleidoscopic palette.

Burk acquaints us with places nestled close to the earth, spots of unparalleled simplicity and surprising impact. Peering through these breezy tangles of grass, we're immediately transported to a place of other-worldly calm that is populated with the magnified sensations of childhood: the perfume of a freshly cut lawn, the thick hum of crickets in the summertime, the swishing lull of leaves from an overhead tree, and grass' singular tickle; all come together to remind us of forgotten outdoor pleasures.

In urging our attention downwards, Burk nudges us backwards, into the soft haze of memory. His perspective could be achieved by an adult who's crouched low to the ground, but otherwise it's the viewpoint of someone very small: a child playing hide-and-seek, pulling himself up from a somersault, or studying a line of marching ants. In this way, Burk ignites our memory, encouraging a wondering curiosity about the subtleties of our surroundings. Perhaps this is how his practice escapes specific classification—the emphasis upon recognition is replaced with the freedom to insert oneself into the coziness of a place not so much seen but rather felt and experienced; this frees us from the constraints of figurative realism. His work's sharp clarity is tempered by the sensuous, fuzzy edges of the memories it recalls.

Burk's close-up perspectives make earth's untamed, essential wildness manageable and navigable. In exploring minutely rendered spaces, we become minutely aware. Though we can't see birds, rabbits, or even beetles in his paintings, we can imagine them, and in doing so we're able to see as a tiny creature might. Burk favors focused visions over sweeping panoramas, encouraging us to establish and foster our own intimate relationships with Nature. Indeed, his economy of subject matter opens up new ways of experiencing an environment that feels inviting and unexplored. Burk's ability to make the wild earth immediately familiar enables him to funnel earth's complexities into radiant and quietly contem-plative spaces.

With austere focus, Charlie Burk analyzes small segments of the wild outdoors, exposing us to Nature in its entirety. His exacting vision reacquaints us with our nuanced world, whose modest patches of grass are conceived as luminously welcoming and vibrantly colorful. Burk's singular brand of realist landscape painting encourages prolonged visual contemplation, and also conveys an appeal for awareness of Nature's hidden charms. These refreshingly uncomplicated paintings transform the experience of walking through a field into something engrossing and rare, possessive of an untamed beauty we feel deeply thankful for. Boundaries of grass give way to the boundless outdoors, whose distant expanses and dazzling colors are quietly, wholly intimated in Burk's paintings. An intimate haven is created in these tightly focused compositions, while the mystery and sacredness of continuous space is conferred and preserved.

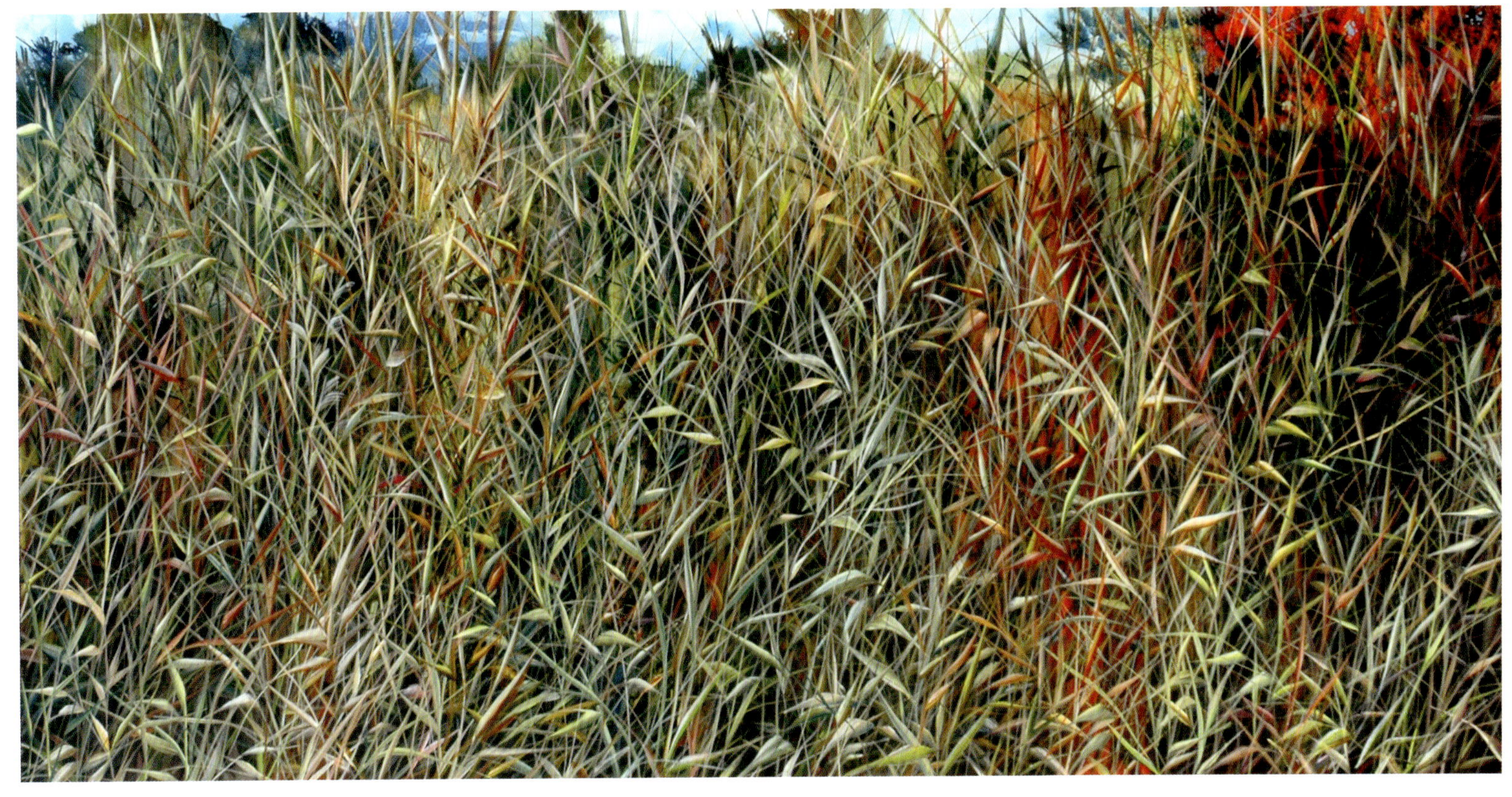

Luxurious Passage, 2014   49 x 97   Oil on panel
Collection of Darlene and David Sillery   45

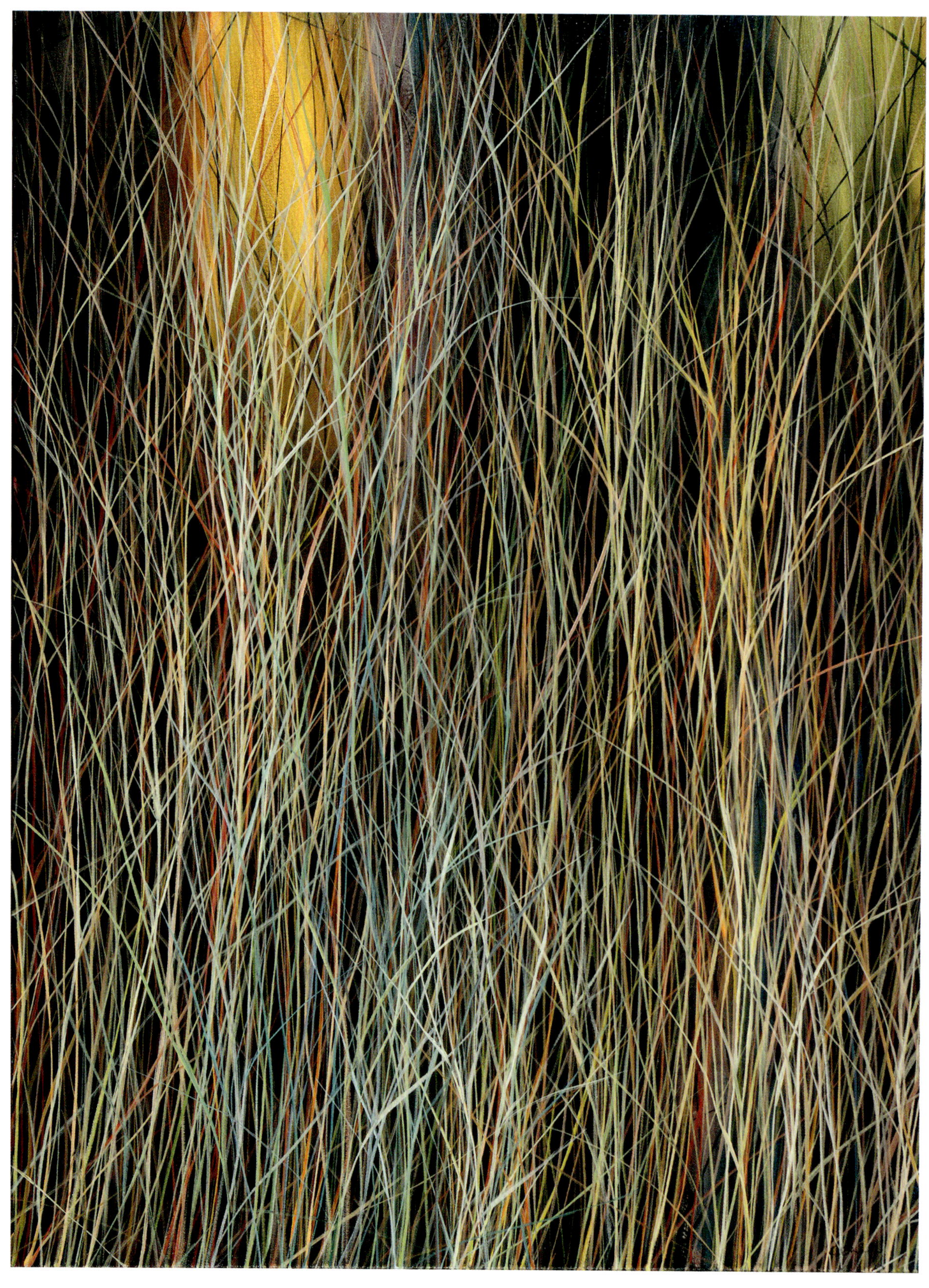

46   *Chorus*, 2018   48 x 36   Oil on canvas

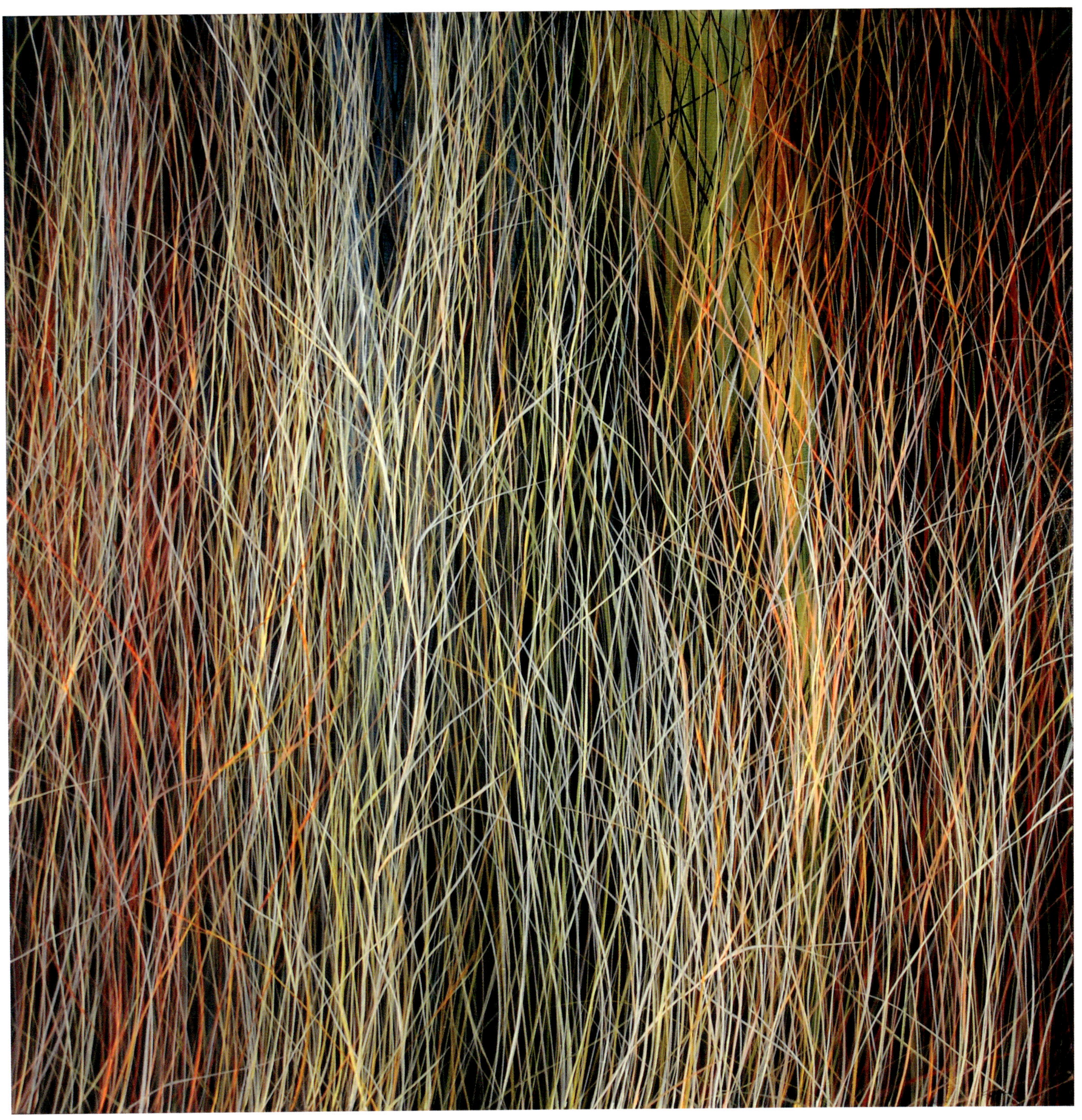

"I am intrigued by the painting process as I work, becoming witness to the multi-faceted, sparkling images-within-images that always arrive. My painting journey for many years has been to begin slowly, start with something abstract, say a color like purple or a horizon, and then it just comes. I am in the zone and I keep working. It's an enigmatic process."

    Essence, 2016   36 x 48   Oil on panel

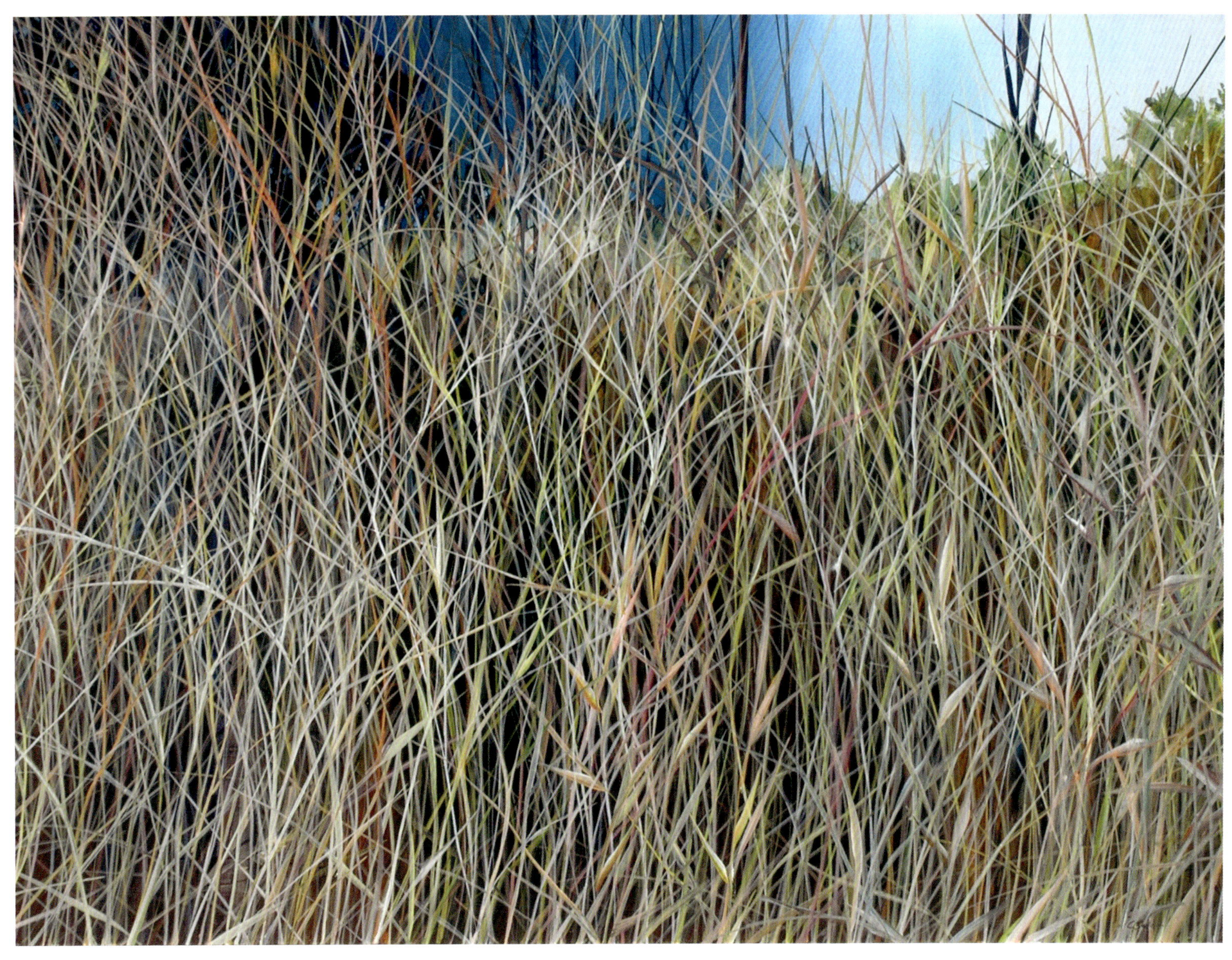

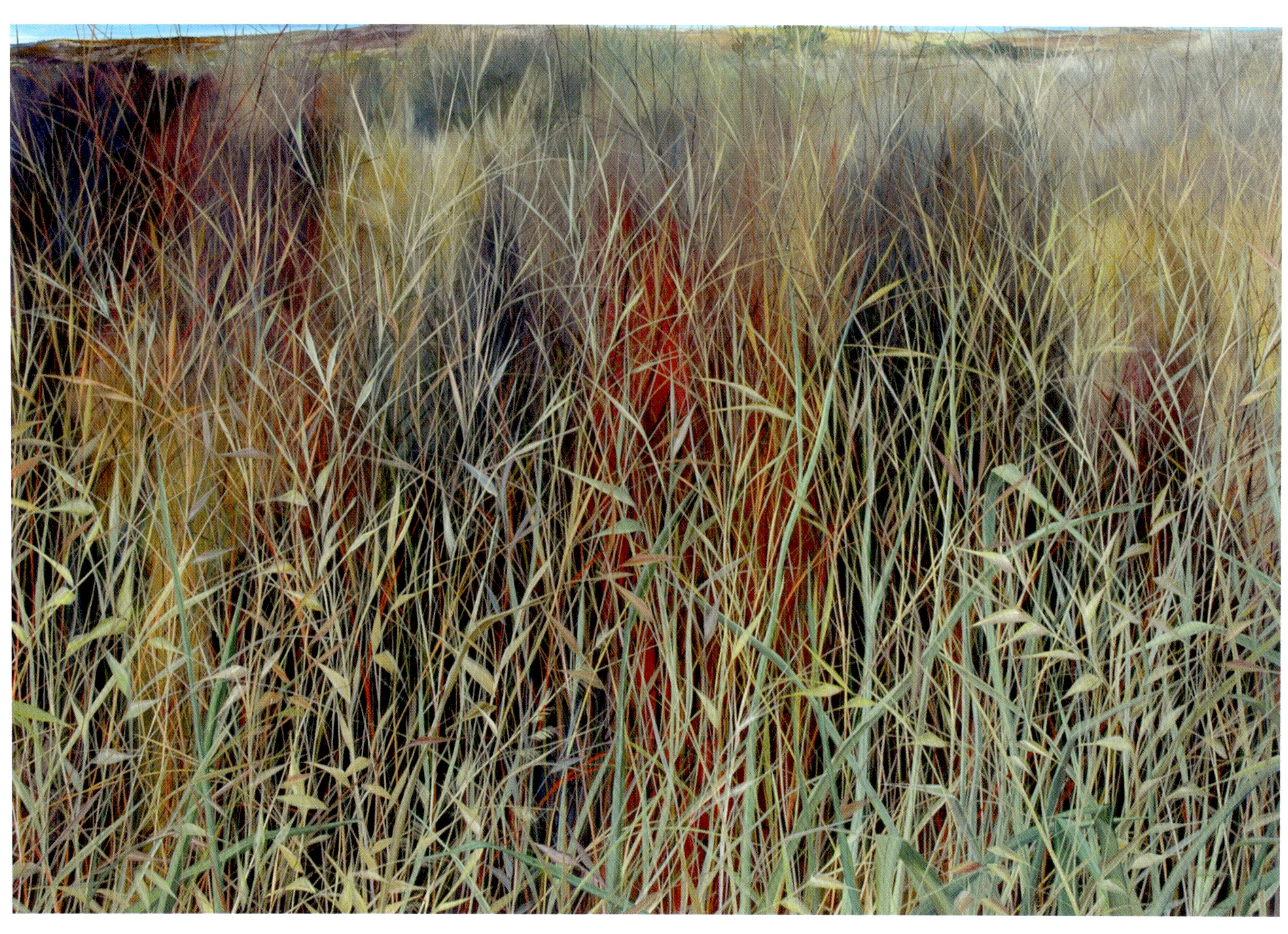

Bountiful Season, 2011   48 x 72   Oil on panel
Collection of Sally Biegert

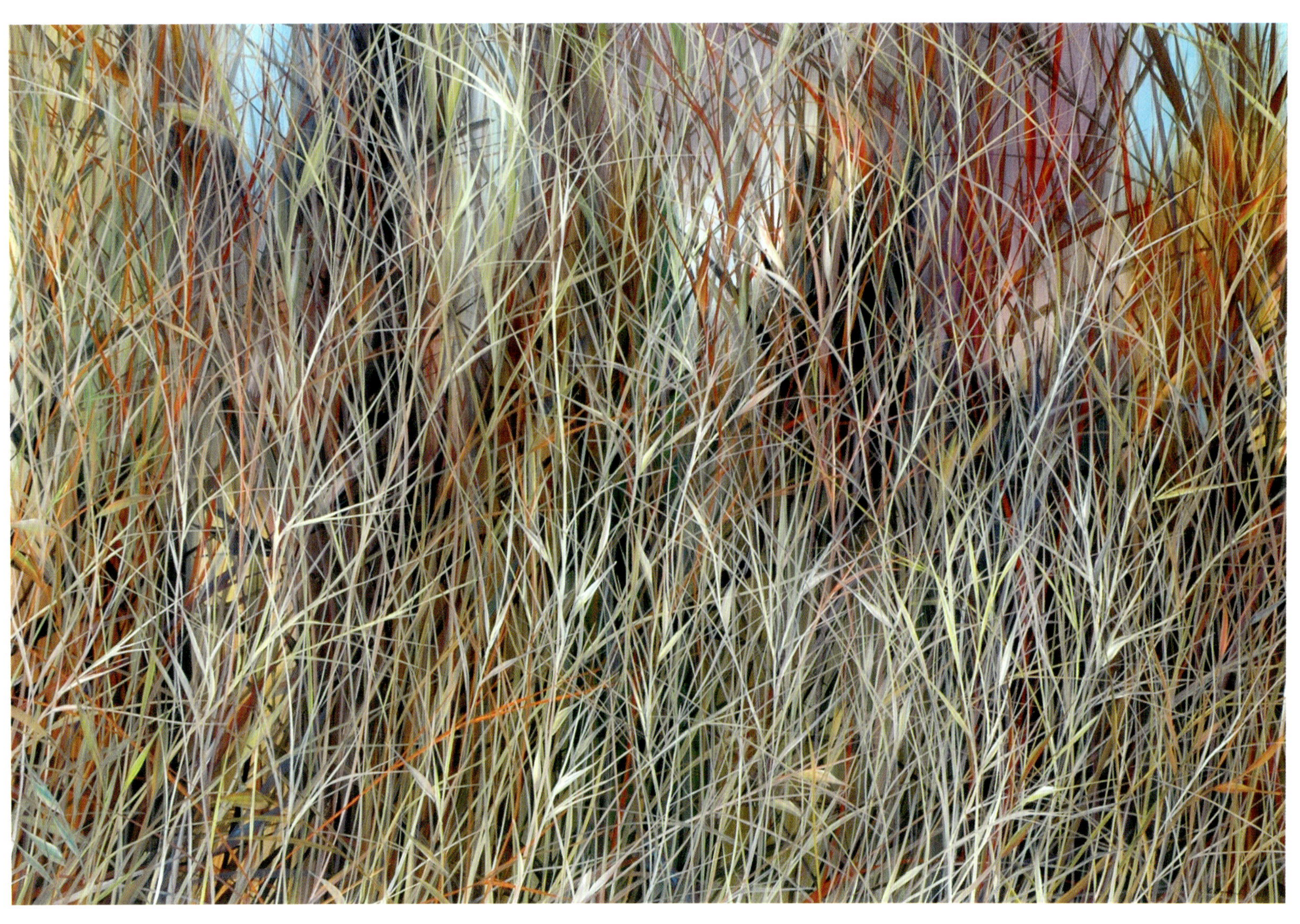

Mystique, 2011   40 x 60   Oil on panel
Collection of Becky and Warren Johnson   51

"I have a dear friend and collector who requested a painting inspired by her West Texas Panhandle landscape. It was to be an unlikely commingling of wide open spaces and my nesting brambles of close up stems. The wispy prairie grasses in this piece evoke the smells and sounds within her native landscape, offering a passage through to the expanse beyond."

Panhandle Grasses, 2010   37 x 57   Oil on panel

    Collection of Cornelia W. Ritchie

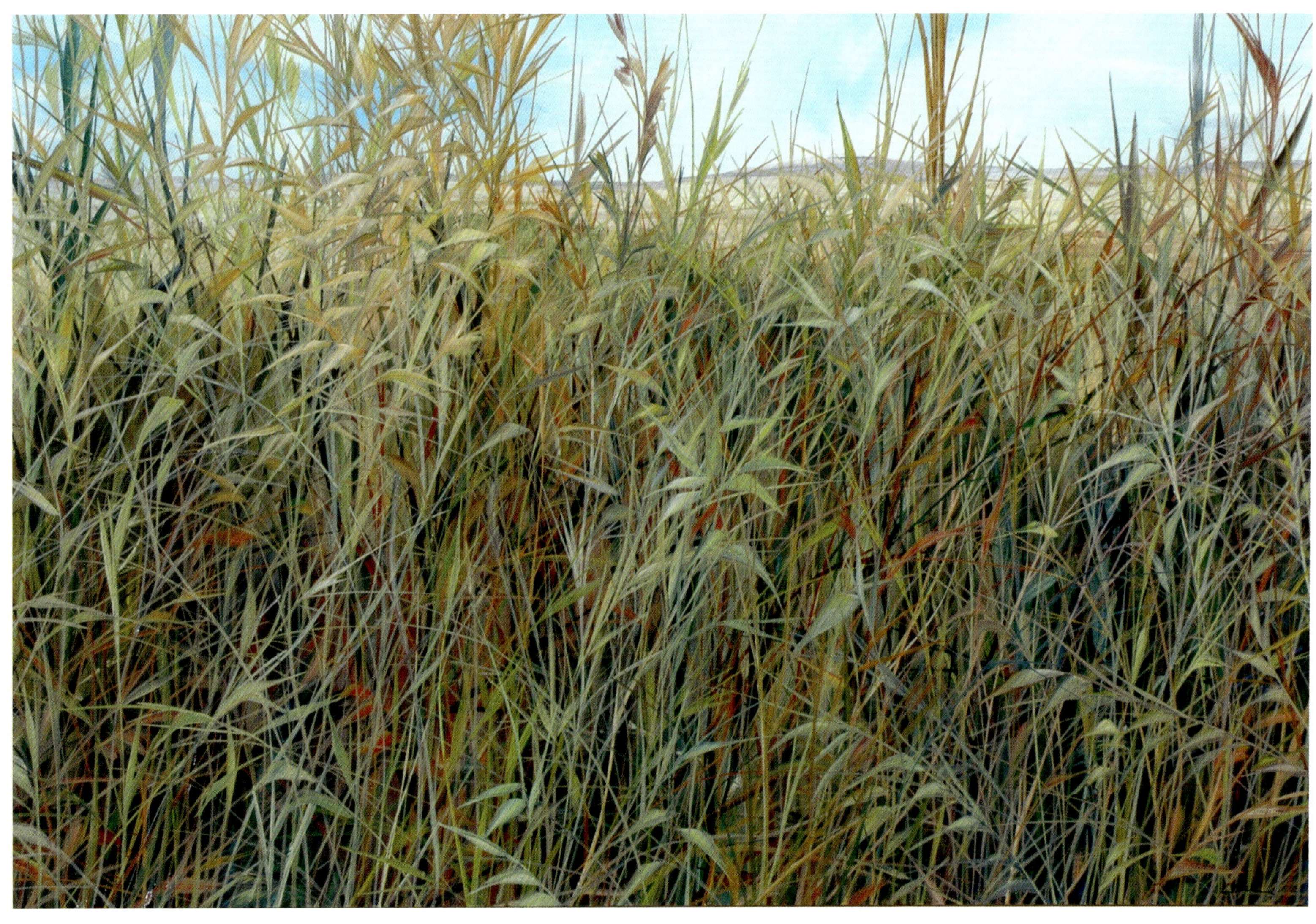

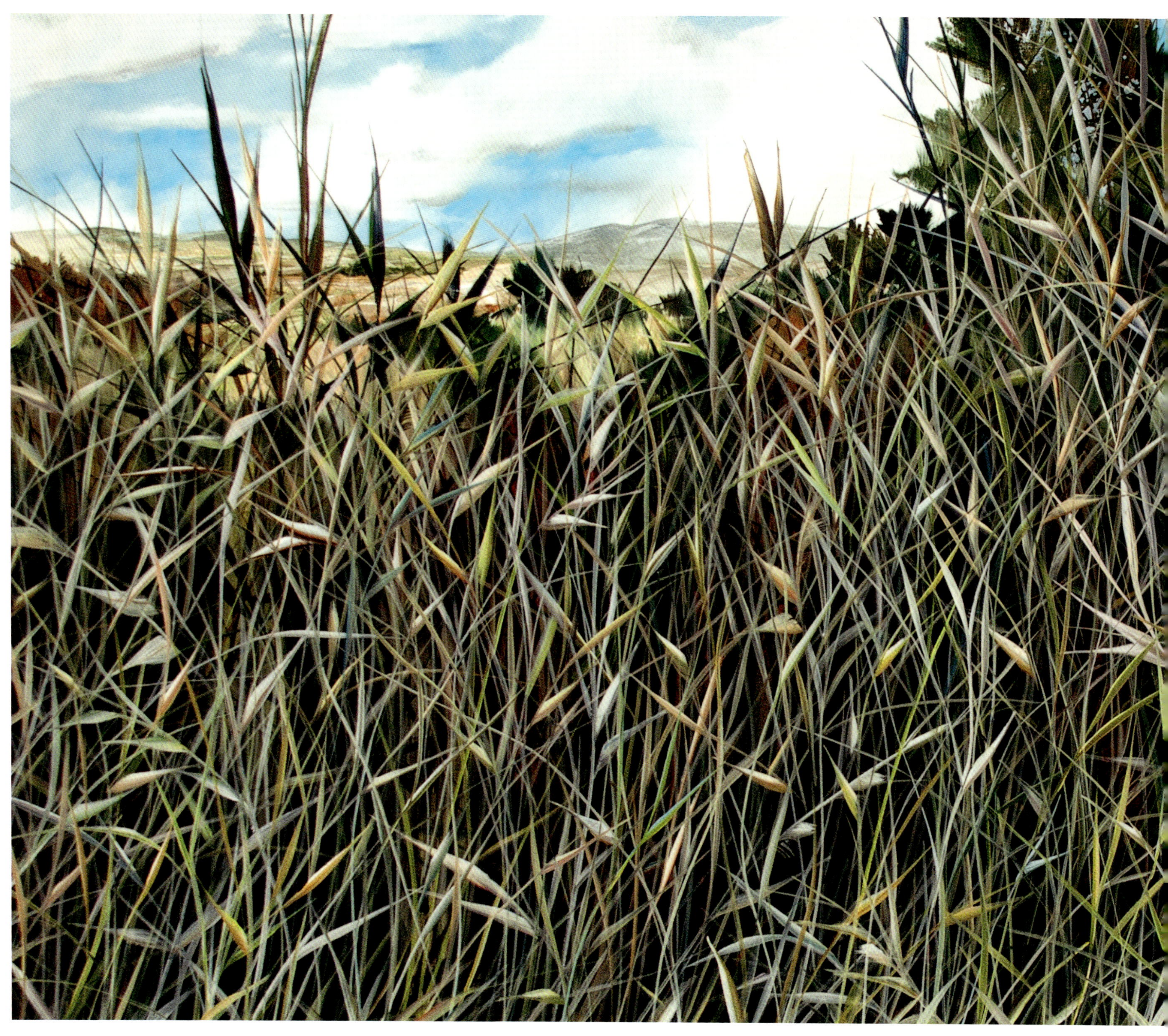

54   *Back to Nature*, 2015   40 x 97   Oil on panel

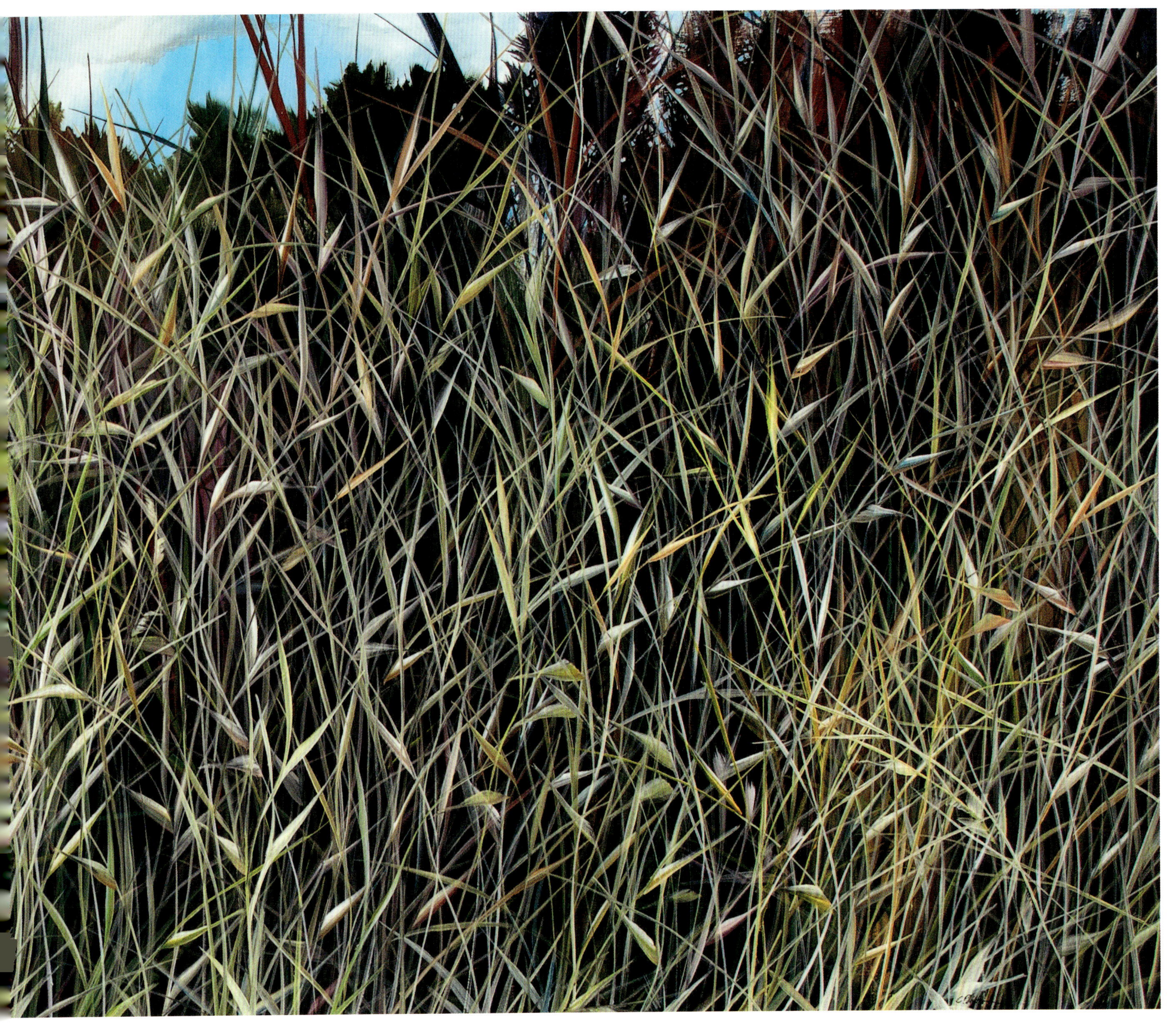

    Far Ahead, 2016   48 x 48   Oil on panel

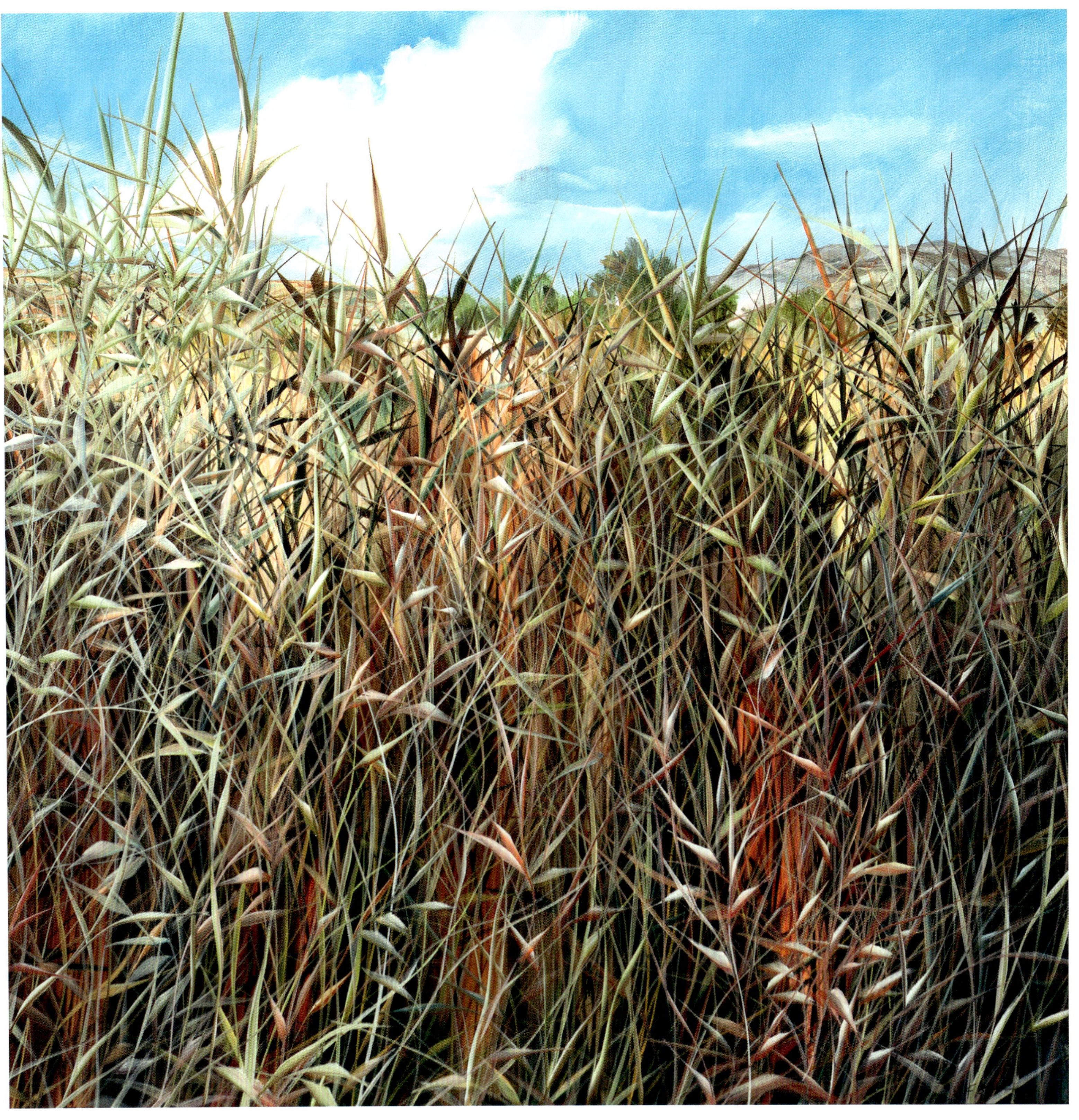

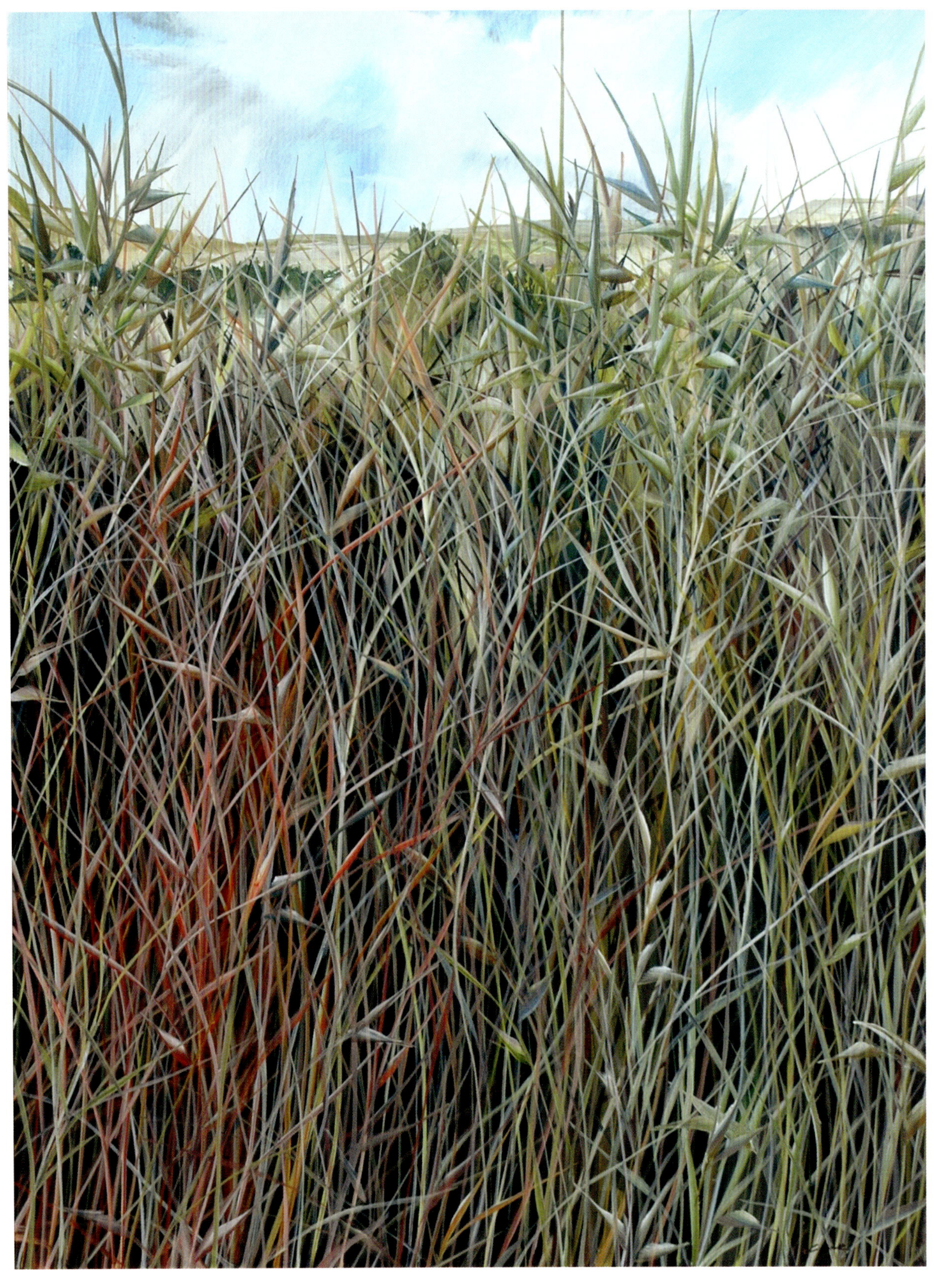

58   *Toward the Horizon, 2016*   48 x 36   Oil on panel

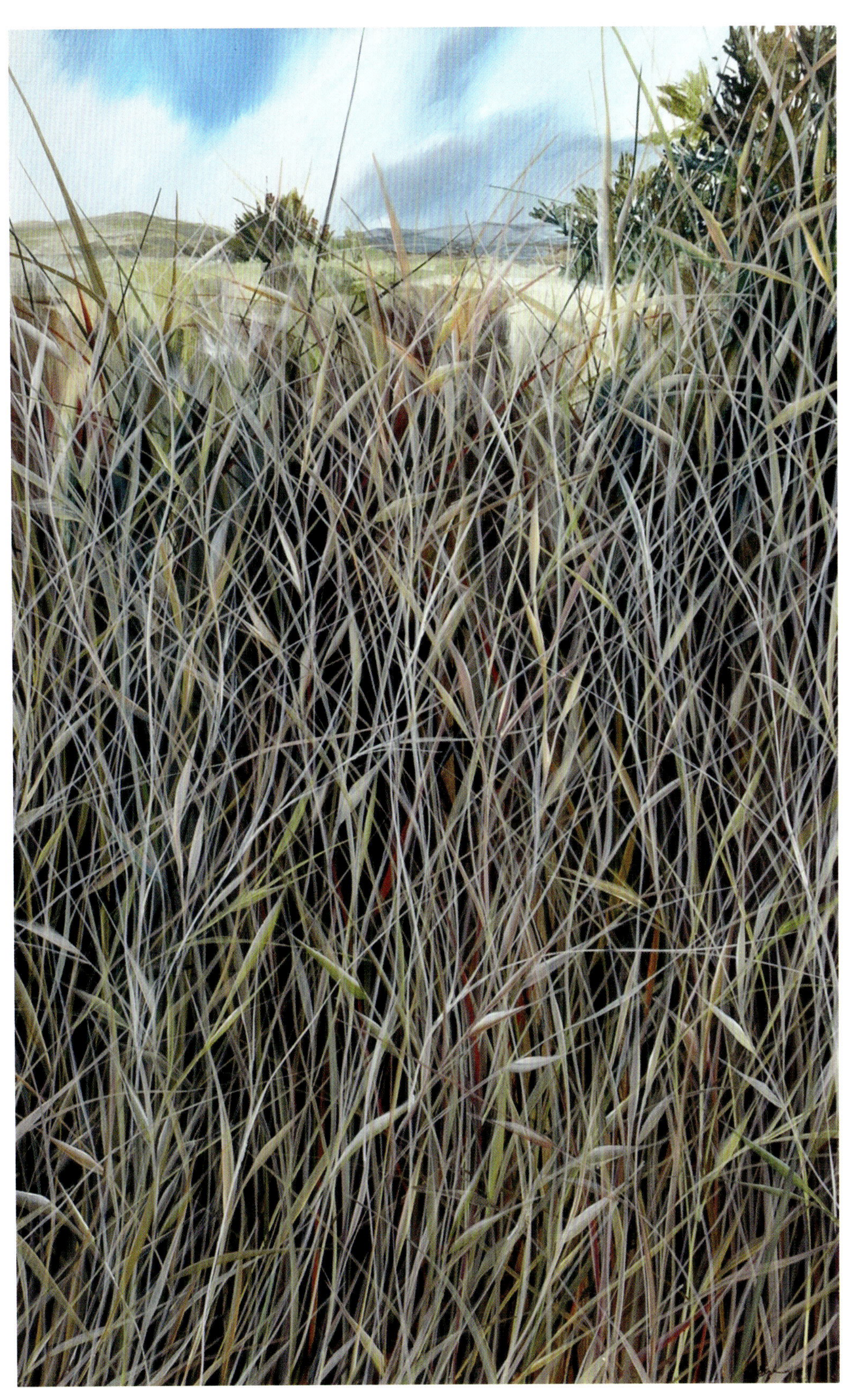

Discovered, 2016   48 x 30   Oil on panel
Collection of Celeste and Michael Van Belle

    Mystical Wanderings, 2016   36 x 36   Oil on panel

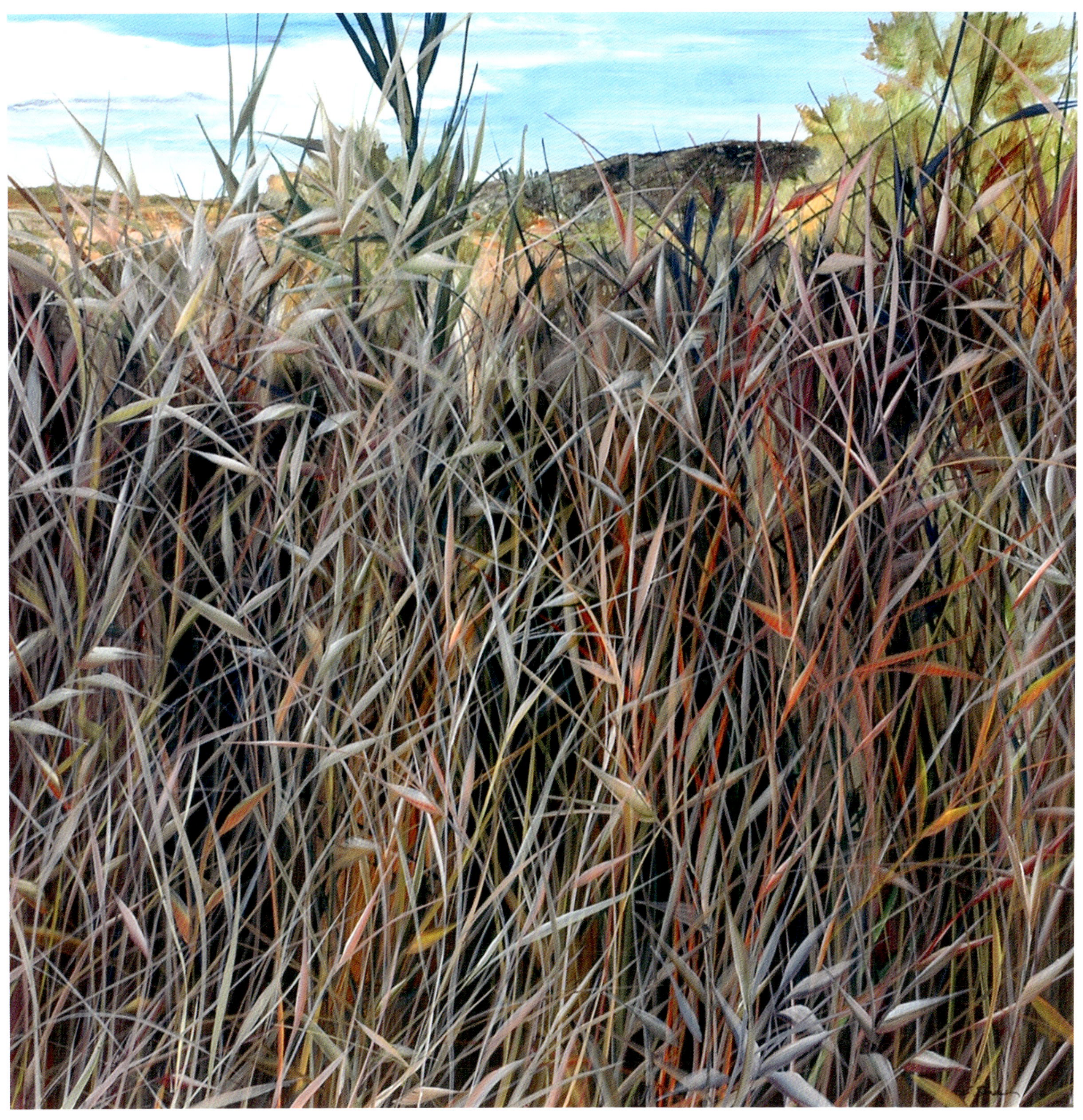

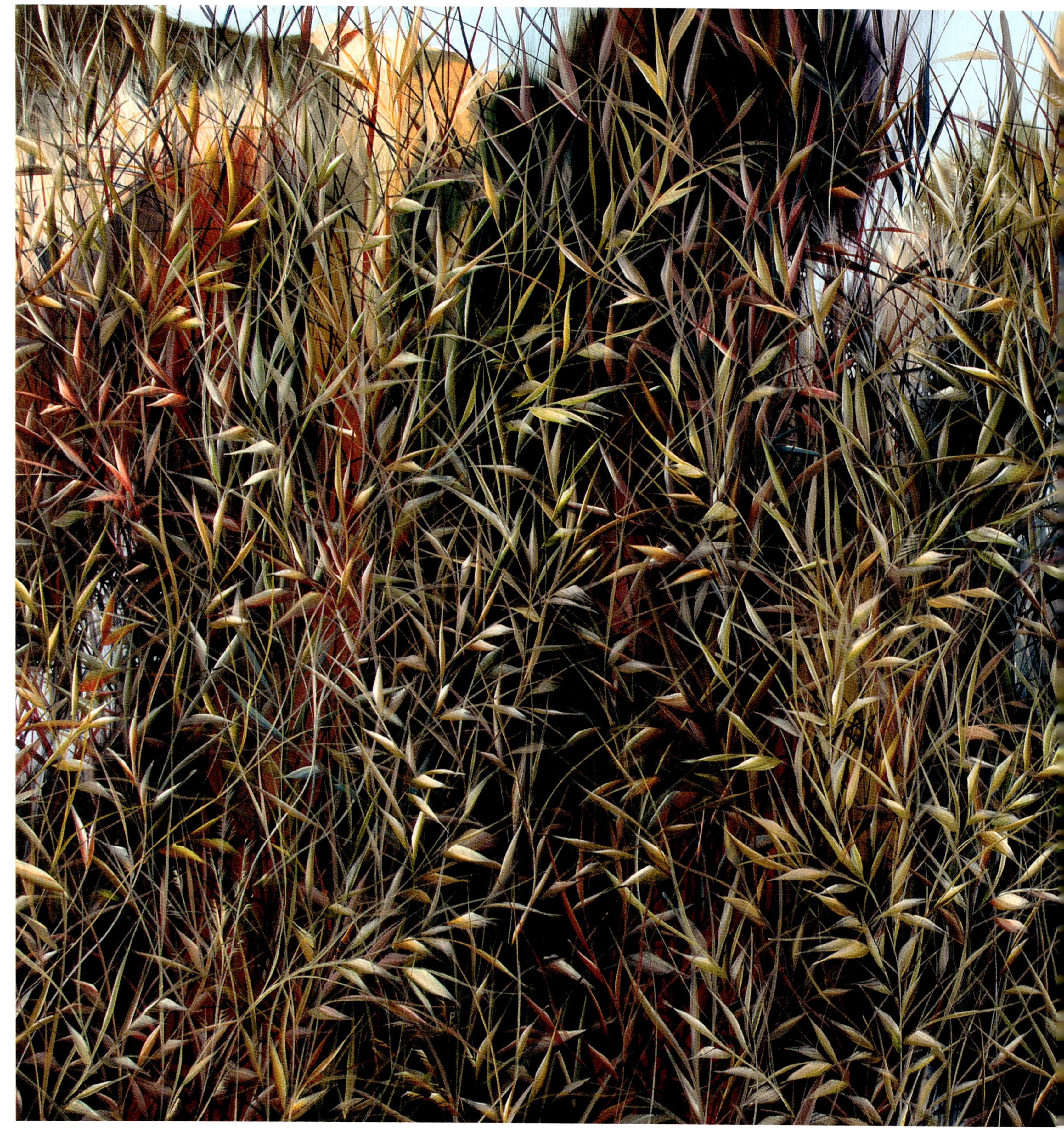

62   *Untamed Beauty*, 2018   49 x 97   Oil on panel

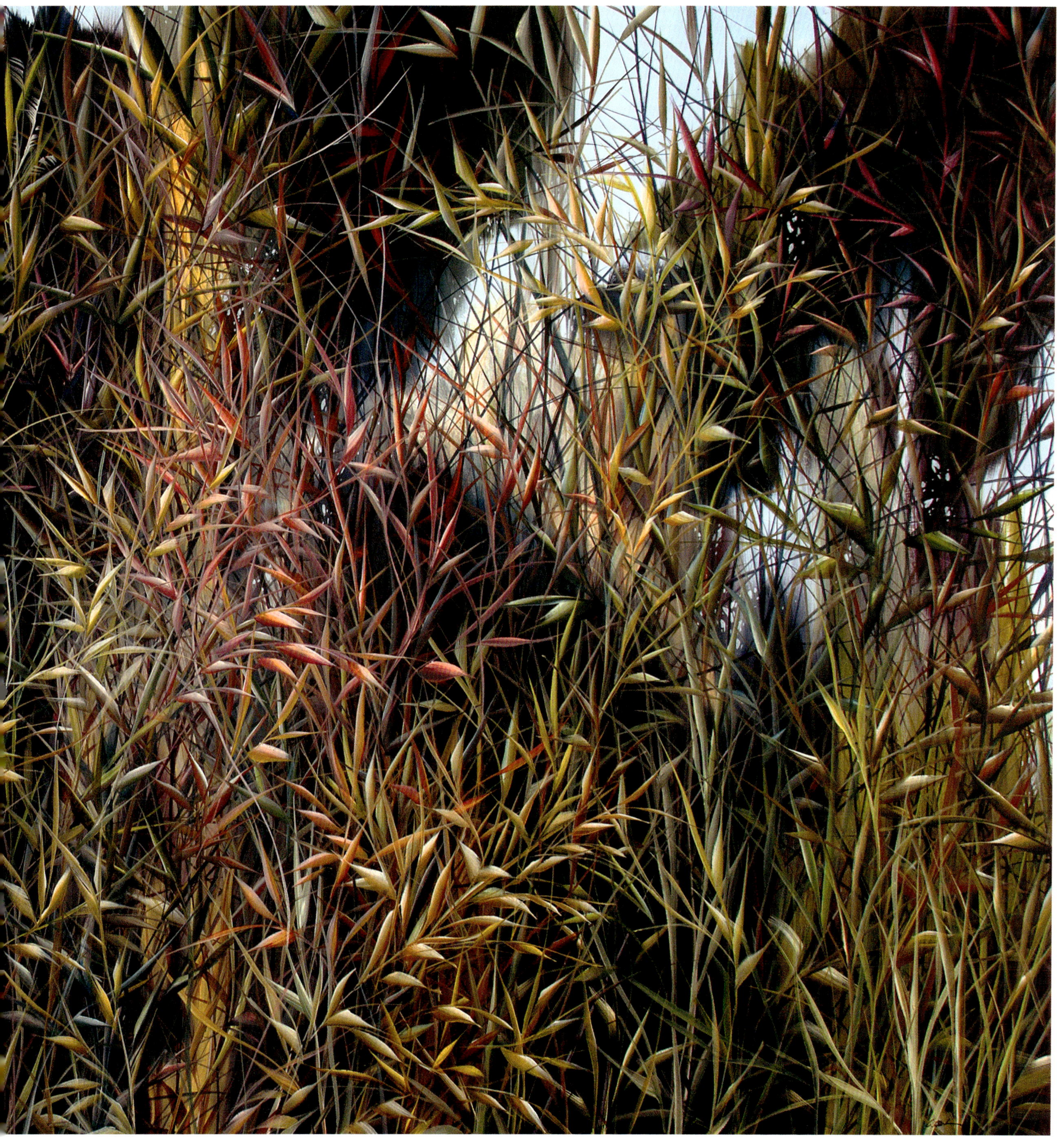

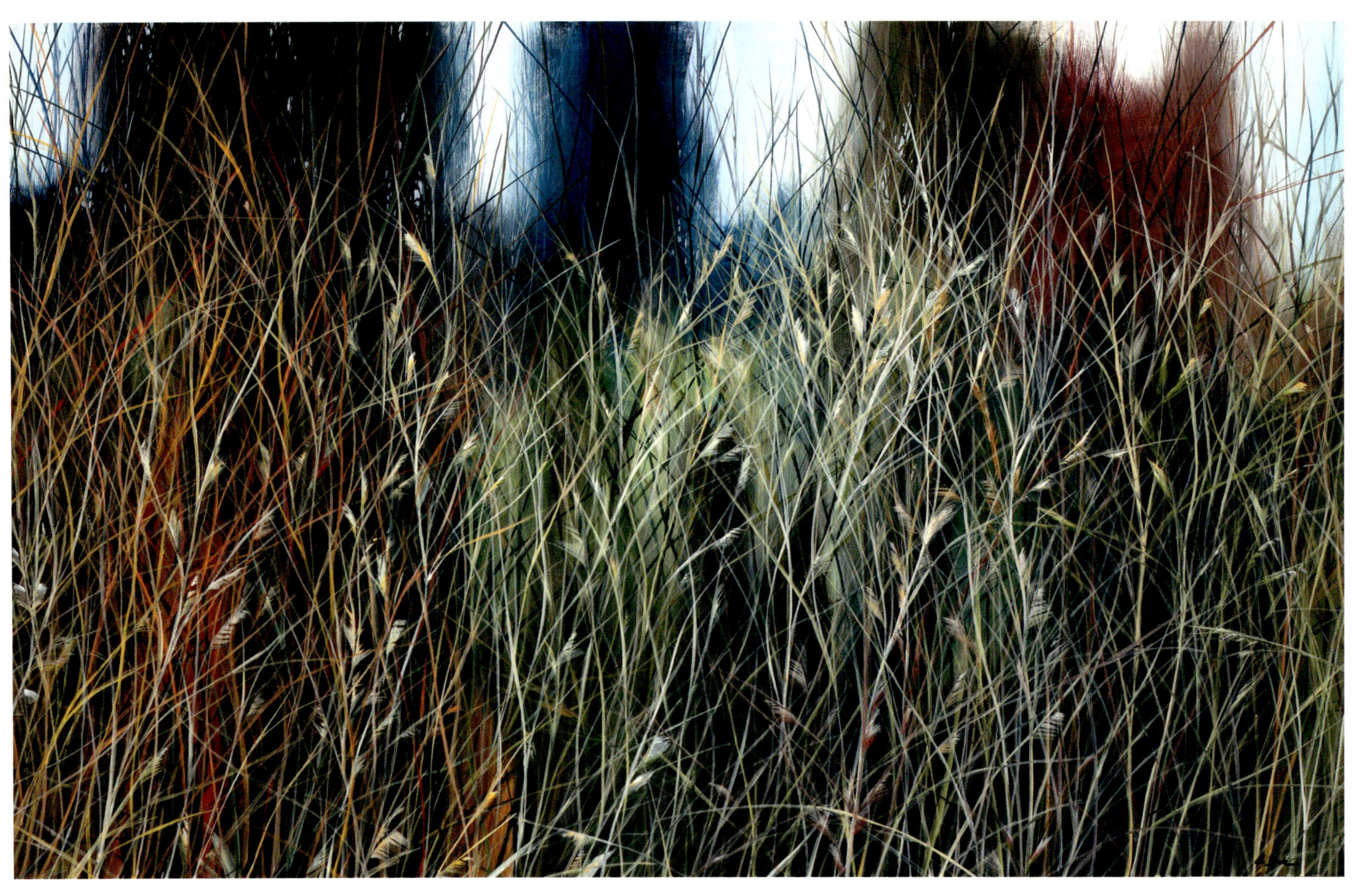

64   *Royal Light Glimmer*, 2017   30 x 48   Oil on panel

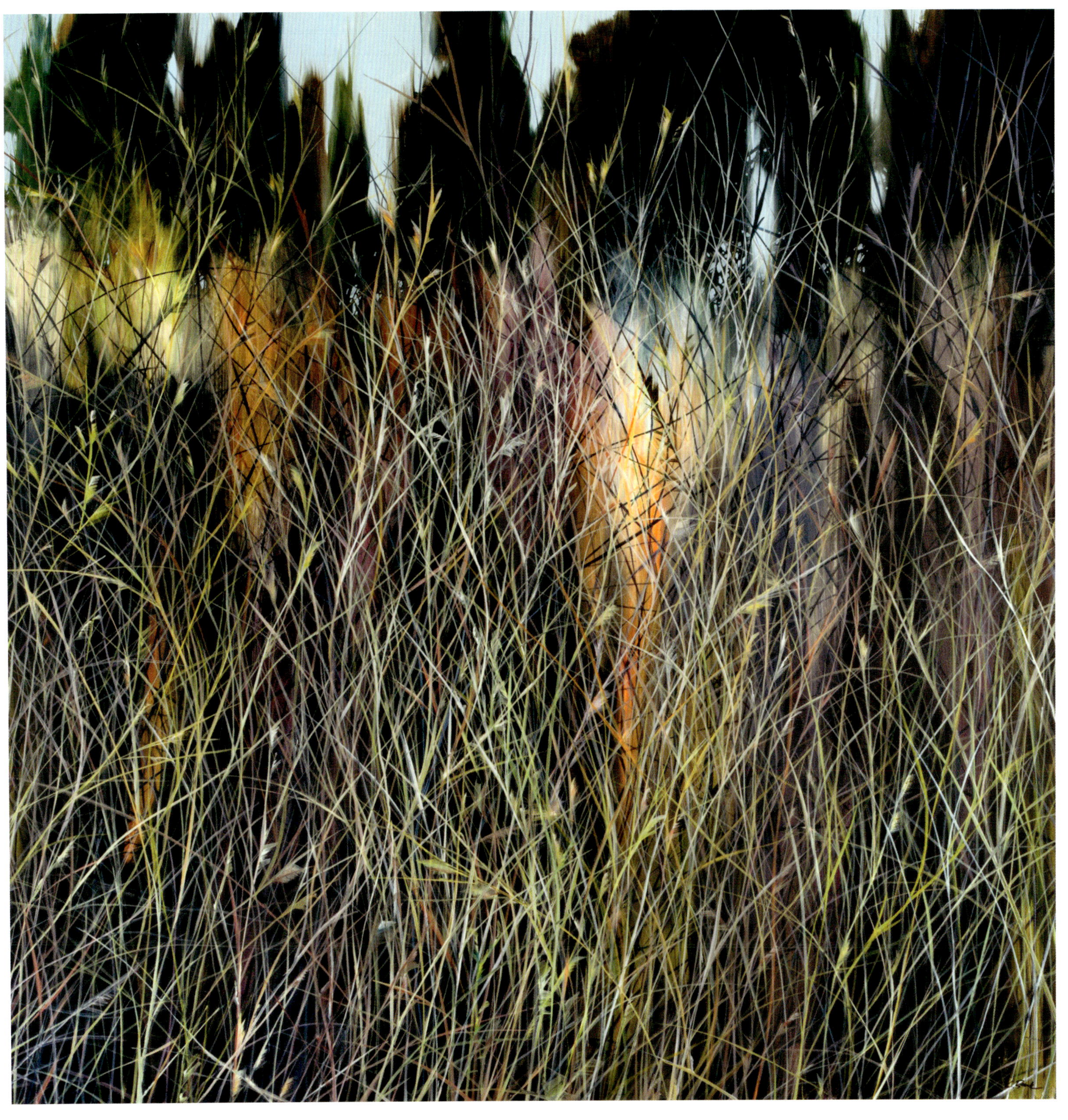

Splendid Sanctuary, 2018   48 x 48   Oil on panel

"Painting became like a weaving, in and out, through and back again, translating what I was viewing into something uniquely mine. I am entranced by surface abstraction, not focusing on a particular scene. My fascination with grasses as a subject intensified and I felt at home."

  Fluttering Blush, 2018   40 x 40   Oil on panel

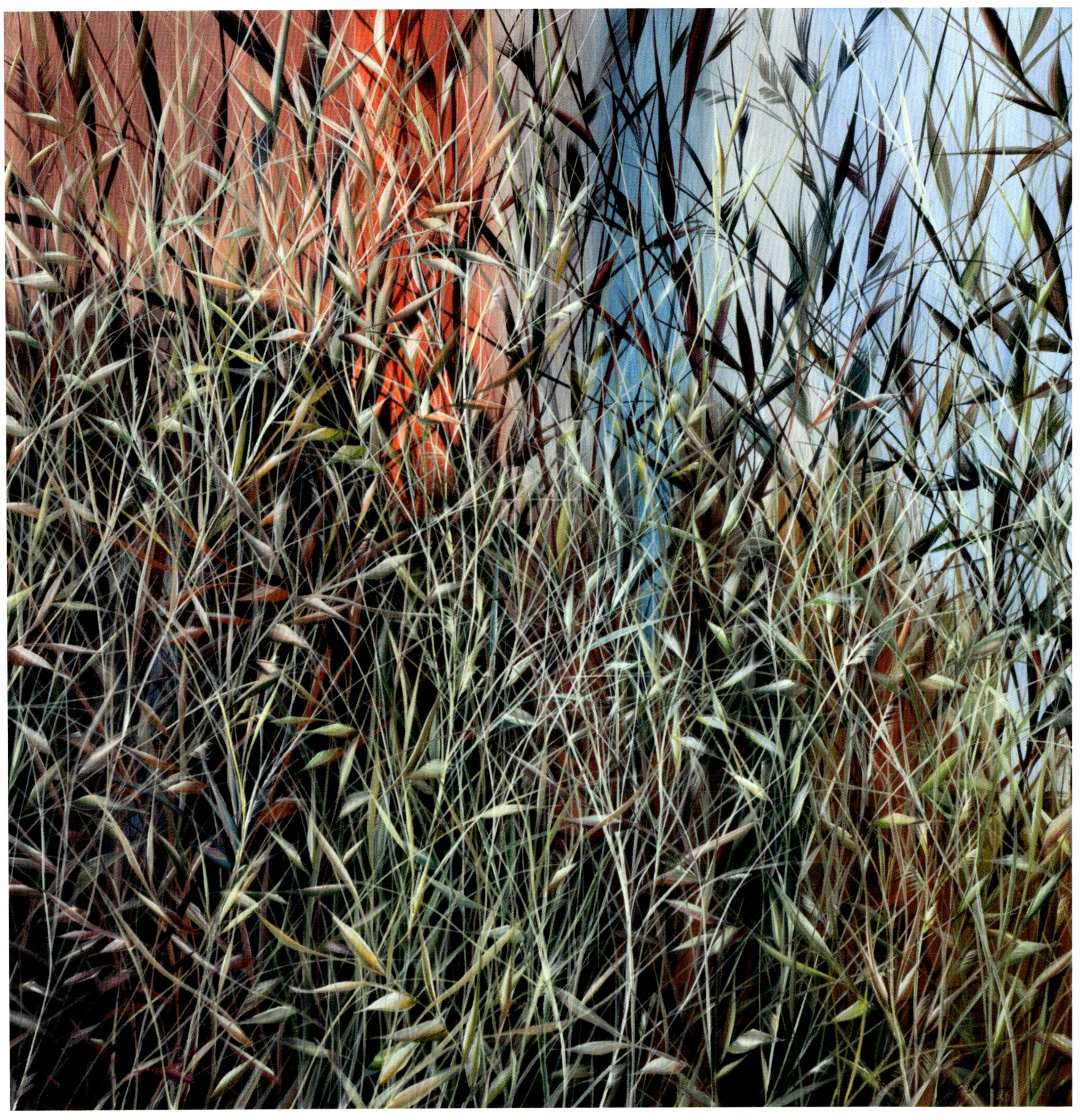

"My most recent paintings may be less abstract and more introspective. No matter the painting's beginnings, I soon am caught up in the weaving and layering process. Is this a vehicle to abstract painting, or is it about access to a hidden reality? The glimpsed horizons and vistas give the image depth, as do the dark voids in the grass texture. A peek at a recognizable reality promotes familiarity and comfort with the image, but the activity is pure painting. It is not an attempt to replicate any real place or time in space."

    My Private World, 2018   60 x 42   Oil on panel

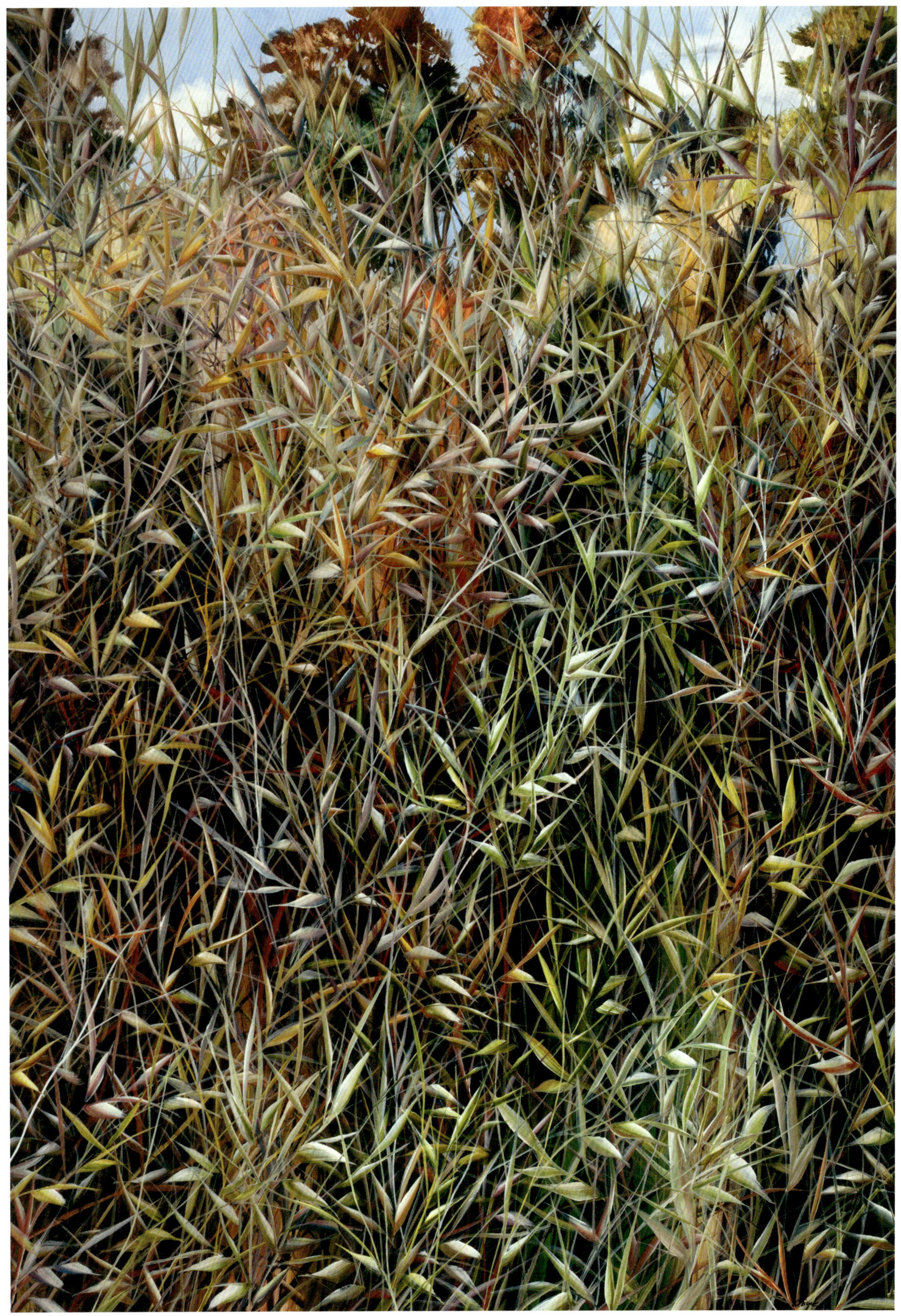

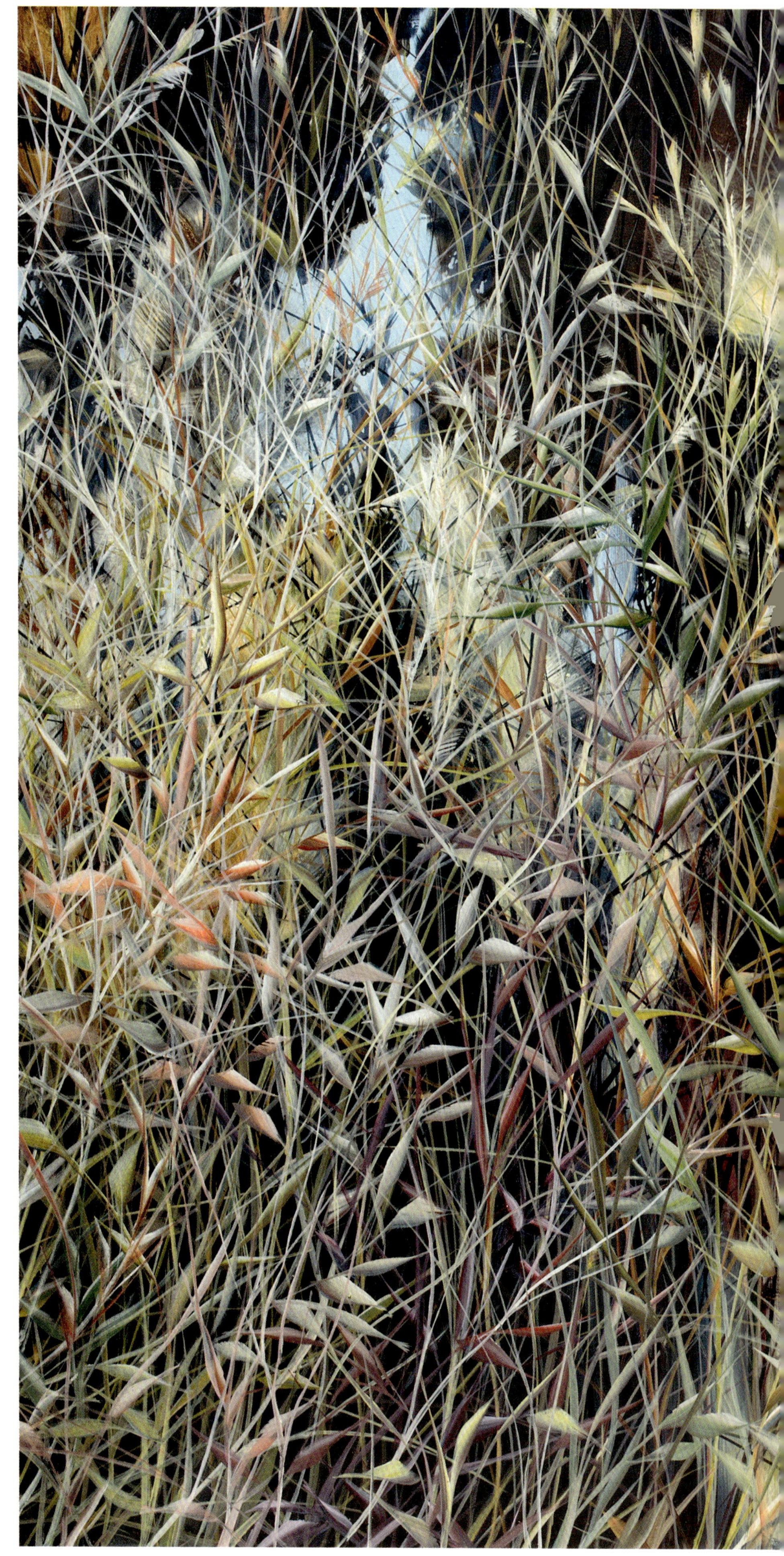

70   *Into the Wonder*, 2018   48 x 72   Oil on panel

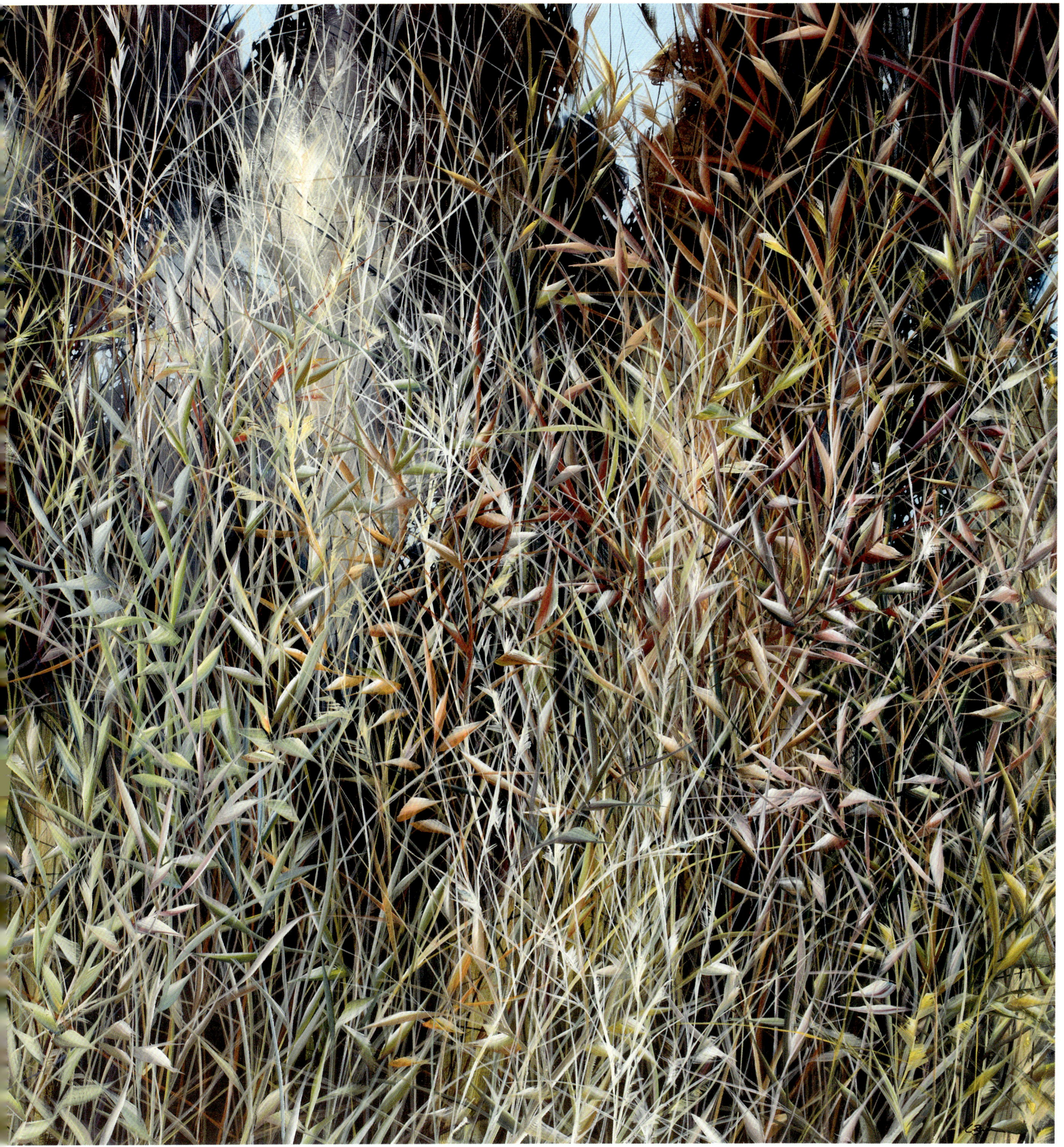

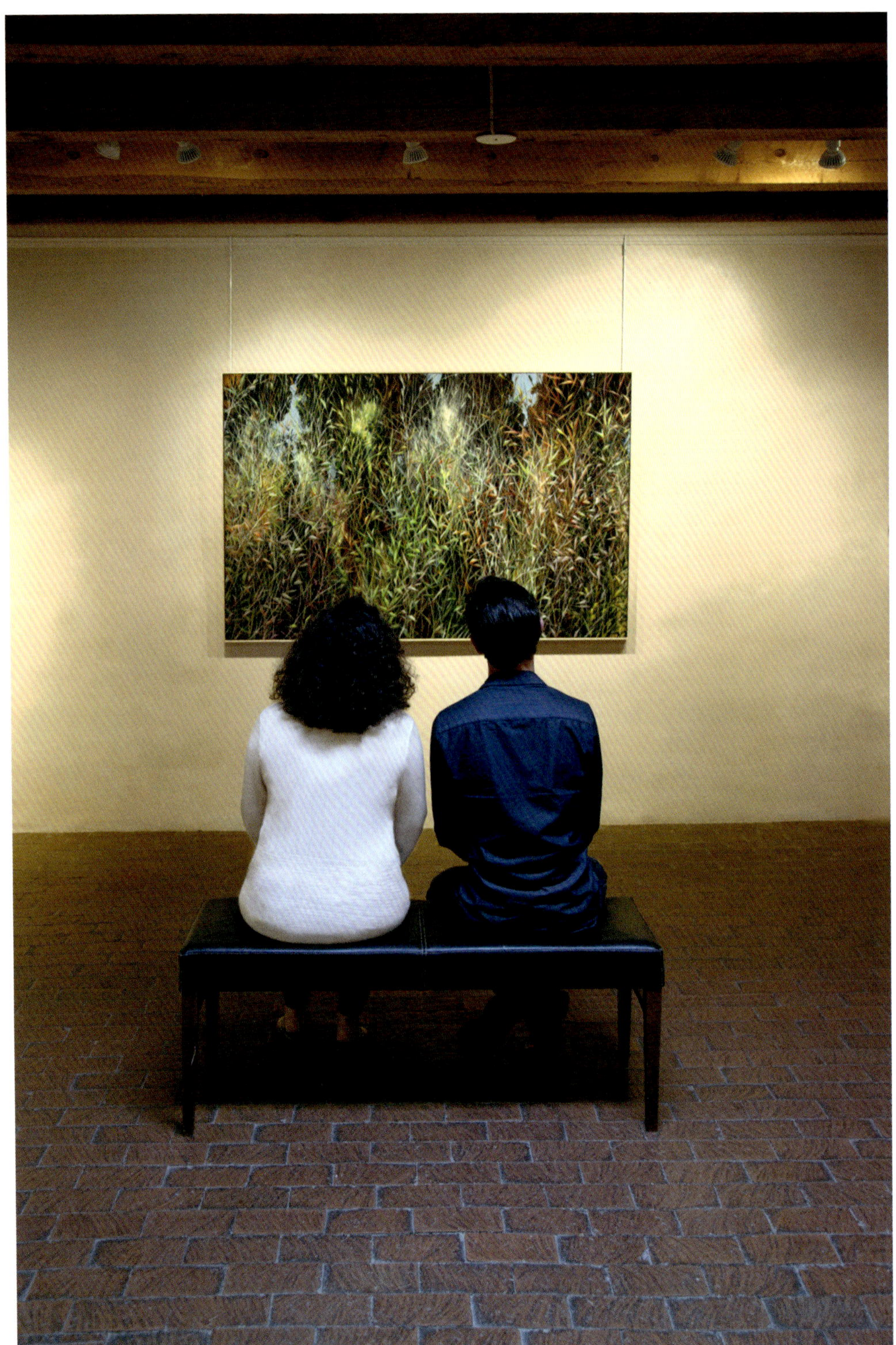

LIST OF WORKS

13   *Afternoon Subsequent to a Modest Success*, 1983   11½ x 19   Watercolor
54   *Back to Nature*, 2015   40 x 97   Oil on panel
33   *Bosque Thicket*, 2008   48 x 48   Oil on panel
50   *Bountiful Season*, 2011   48 x 72   Oil on panel
46   *Chorus*, 2018   48 x 36   Oil on canvas
10   *Confessional*, 1992   30 x 22   Watercolor
34   *Cool Reflection*, 2016   49 x 19   Oil on panel
 6   *Dancing Light*, 2017   40 x 72   Oil on panel
59   *Discovered*, 2016   48 x 30   Oil on panel
49   *Essence*, 2016   36 x 48   Oil on panel
57   *Far Ahead*, 2016   48 x 48   Oil on panel
35   *Fireflies*, 2009   30 x 48   Oil on panel
67   *Fluttering Blush*, 2018   40 x 40   Oil on panel
43   *Garden Song*, 2014   12 x 12   Oil on panel
39   *Grace I*, 2009   42 x 42   Oil on panel
71   *Into the Wonder*, 2018   48 x 72   Oil on panel
45   *Luxurious Passage*, 2014   49 x 97   Oil on panel
42   *Lyric Afternoon*, 2015   32 x 49   Oil on panel
40   *Morning Glow*, 2013   30 x 40   Oil on panel
69   *My Private World*, 2018   60 x 42   Oil on panel
61   *Mystical Wanderings*, 2016   36 x 36   Oil on panel
51   *Mystique*, 2011   40 x 60   Oil on panel
37   *Nature's Glory*, 2011   48 x 96   Oil on panel
53   *Panhandle Grasses*, 2010   37 x 57   Oil on panel
64   *Royal Light Glimmer*, 2017   30 x 48   Oil on panel
15   *Saw Horse, Barrel and Tires*, 1985   15 x 22   Watercolor
19   *Site of an Unattended Montana Picnic*, 1992   22⅓ x 35   Watercolor
65   *Splendid Sanctuary*, 2018   48 x 48   Oil on panel
17   *Square Entry*, 1990   40 x 40   Watercolor
12   *Store Front*, 1981   15 x 22   Watercolor
29   *Summer Jazz*, 2007   48 x 96   Oil on panel
 9   *Sundance*, 2012   72 x 96   Oil on canvas
58   *Toward the Horizon*, 2016   48 x 36   Oil on panel
47   *Tribute*, 2018   60 x 60   Oil on canvas
62   *Untamed Beauty*, 2018   49 x 97   Oil on panel
23   *Untitled I*, 2004   48 x 48   Oil on panel
25   *Untitled XXXXV*, 2005   48 x 96   Oil on panel
26   *Untitled No. 83*, 2006   24 x 48   Oil on panel
27   *Warm Afternoon*, 2006   60 x 48   Oil on panel
14   *Wood and Wire*, 1985   20 x 30   Watercolor

        Cover Image: Into the Wonder, 2018   48 x 72   Oil on panel

CURRICULUM VITAE

Charlie Burk
b. 1947, Albuquerque, NM
1973, BFA, University of New Mexico, Albuquerque, NM

EXHIBITIONS

2018 Solo Exhibition, Winterowd Fine Art, Santa Fe, NM
2017 SOFA Chicago, Art Fair, Chicago, IL
      Winterowd Fine Art, *Colorful Summer*, Santa Fe, NM
2016 SOFA Chicago, Art Fair, Chicago, IL
2015 Affordable Art Fair NYC, Metropolitan Pavilion, New York, NY
2014 LA Art Show, Los Angeles, CA (also 2013)
2013 *Changing Perceptions of the Western Landscape*,
      Albuquerque Museum of Art and History, Albuquerque, NM
      Curator Andrew Connors
2012 AAF Contemporary Art Fair, Seattle, WA
2011 Art Chicago 2011, Merchandise Mart, Chicago, IL
      San Francisco Fine Art Fair, Fort Mason Center, San Francisco, CA
2010 *Albuquerque Now*, Albuquerque Museum of Art and History,
      Albuquerque, NM
      Artrageous, Palm Springs Art Museum, Palm Springs, CA
      AAF Contemporary Art Fair, New York, NY
      Group Exhibition, Hayden Hayes Gallery, Colorado Springs, CO
2009 *High Tide/Low Grasses*, 725 Project Space, Santa Fe, NM
      Red Dot Miami Art Show, Miami, FL
      ART Santa Fe, Santa Fe, NM
2008 Solo Exhibition, Winterowd Fine Art, Santa Fe, NM
      AAF Contemporary Art Fair, Metropolitan Pavilion, NY, NY
      (also 2007)
2007 *Out West*, curated group exhibition touring 10 cities in China
      Art Now Miami, concurrent exhibition w/ ART Basel
      Miami Beach, FL
      Gallery Artists Showcase, Leslie Levy Gallery, Scottsdale AZ
2006 Solo Exhibition, Winterowd Fine Art, Santa Fe, NM
      AAF Contemporary Art Fair, Pier 92, New York, NY
      (also 2004 & 2005)
      Group Exhibition, Leslie Levy Gallery, Scottsdale, AZ (also 2005)
2005 Group Show, Winterowd Fine Art, Santa Fe, NM
      Emerging Artists Show, Parada Hall, Scottsdale, AZ

2004 Inaugural Exhibition, Winterowd Fine Art, Santa Fe, NM
2003 *Stems and Seeds*, Solo Exhibition, Rick Moore Gallery,
      Santa Fe, NM
      Small Is Beautiful, Karan Ruhlen Gallery, Santa Fe, NM
2001 *A Show with Heart*, Joyce Robins Gallery, Santa Fe, NM
2000 *Just Originals*, Corporate Offices Gallery, Albuquerque, NM
1999 *101 Cup Show*, Karan Ruhlen Gallery, Santa Fe, NM
      (also 1997 & 1998)
1997 Rocky Mountain National, (award), Golden, CO
      (also 1976, 1979, 1980, 1982 & 1985)
1991 *Charlie Burk*, Solo Exhibition, Kyra Hidalgo, Houston, TX
1990 Two-person show, Alpha Gallery, Denver, CO
      Artists of the Southwest, Somerstown Gallery, Somers, NY
1989 *Charlie Burk*, Solo Exhibition, Laurel Seth Gallery, Santa Fe, NM
      Two-person show, Albuquerque Academy Gallery,
       Albuquerque, NM
1987 Gallery exhibition, Austin Gallery, Scottsdale, AZ (also 1986)
1984 *Charlie Burk*, Solo Exhibition, Iman Galleries, San Angelo, TX
1983-84
      Art and the Law, traveling national exhibit sponsored by
      West Publishing
1982 Watercolor USA, Springfield Art Museum, MO (award)
      (also, 1977 & 1980)
1981 *Charlie Burk*, Solo Exhibition, Kimball Art Center, Park City, UT
      Western Federation of Watercolor Society, Corpus Christi, TX
      (award)
1979 American Watercolor Society, New York, NY
1977 *Watercolor in New Mexico*, NM Museum of Fine Arts,
      Santa Fe, NM
1976 *Allied Artists of America's Exhibition*, New York, NY

COLLECTIONS

Albuquerque Museum, Albuquerque, NM
Texas Instruments
Bank of America
Intel Corporation
Guadalupe County Courthouse, Santa Rosa, NM
Okay Owingee Pueblo Tribal Council, NM
Blackberry Farm Corp, Knoxville, TN
Wildlife Trading Co, Ridgefield, CT
City of Las Cruces, NM
Blue Mesa, Albuquerque, NM
Lovelace Clinic, Albuquerque, NM
MJG Corporation, Albuquerque, NM
Sandia Laboratory, Albuquerque, NM
City of Albuquerque, Albuquerque, NM
States Steamship Company, San Francisco, CA
(72 paintings) Ships: SS Arizona, SS Maine, SS Nevada & SS Illinois
and numerous private collections

SELECTED PUBLICATIONS

2018   Charlie Burk, Fresco Books
2014   Trend Magazine, fall
2009   Low Tide/Tall Grasses catalog
2008   Southwest Art (also 2005 & 2006)
2008   Santa Fean, feature article
2007   FOCUS Magazine, feature article
2005   Art & Antiques, article
1994   Albuquerque Monthly Magazine, feature article
1989   Albuquerque Journal, feature article
1986   Santa Fe Lifestyle Magazine, feature article
1982   Contemporary Western Artists by Harold & Peggy Samuels
1979   Southwest Art Magazine, feature article